wholesome
kitchen

delicious recipes with beans, lentils,
grains, and other natural foods

Ross Dobson

photography by Peter Cassidy

RYLAND
PETERS
& SMALL

LONDON NEW YORK

Dedication

To Mum and Dad. For being my most
loyal customers. It wouldn't be Saturday
without you at the café.

**Design and Photographic
Art Direction**
    Steve Painter

Senior Commissioning Editor
    Julia Charles

Production Toby Marshall

Publishing Director Alison Starling

Art Director Leslie Harrington

Food Stylist Lizzie Harris

Prop Stylist Róisín Nield

Indexer Vanessa Bird

Author's Acknowledgments

Thanks again to all the crew at Ryland
Peters & Small for the opportunity to
work on another wonderful project.
I really missed being in the UK this
year but cherished this opportunity.

First published in the United States
in 2010 by Ryland Peters & Small, Inc
519 Broadway, 5th Floor
New York, NY 10012
www.rylandpeters.com

10 9 8 7 6 5 4 3 2 1

ISBN: 978 1 84975 035 6

Library of Congress Cataloging-in-
Publication Data

Dobson, Ross, 1965-

  Wholesome kitchen : delicious recipes
beans, lentils, grains, and other natural
foods / Ross Dobson ; photography by
Peter Cassidy.
    p. cm.
  Includes index.
  ISBN 978-1-84975-035-6
  1. Cookery (Natural foods) I. Title.
  TX741.D623 2010
  641.5'636--dc22

2010017909

Printed and bound in China.

Notes

• All spoon measurements are level
unless otherwise specified.

• Eggs are large unless otherwise
specified. Uncooked or partially cooked
eggs should not be served to the very
old, frail, young children, pregnant
women, or those with compromised
immune systems.

• When a recipe calls for the grated peel
of lemons or limes, buy unwaxed fruit
and wash well before using. If you can
only find treated fruit, scrub well in
warm, soapy water before using.

• Ovens should be preheated to the
specified temperature. Recipes in this
book were tested using a regular oven.
If using a fan-assisted oven, follow the
manufacturer's instructions for adjusting
temperatures.

CONTENTS

the world's healthiest foods

Beans, lentils, peas, and grains have been the most important staple foods in just about every corner of the globe since man first grew and harvested crops. They are nutritious and delicious and can be cooked in hundreds of different and exciting ways to create healthy, satisfying meals. In recent years, more and more interesting and unusual varieties have become available and these make a great addition to any modern cook's repertoire, mine included! Also, as our desire to try new flavors and embrace ideas from cultures other than our own grows, we learn more about the incredible range of ways in which these foods can be prepared and enjoyed.

The recipes in this book have been culled from different styles of cooking from around the world and all feature beans, lentils, peas, or grains as their main ingredient (or sometimes a combination of more than one.) From simple dips and soups to exotic curries and richly-flavored casseroles, many of these dishes have ancient roots and there aren't many foods prepared today that have been eaten for thousands of years. For example, Ful Medames (page 13), a simple broad bean dish, was eaten by the pharaohs in Ancient Egypt and is still eaten on the streets of Cairo today.

Pulses are the edible seeds from plants belonging to the legume family, and include chickpeas and a vast array of colorful and tasty beans, from cannellini to pinto. Simple to prepare and sustaining they have been enjoyed for millennia, by kings and peasants alike. As a convenience food they tick plenty of boxes. Once dried they have a very long shelf life and water is all that's required to cook them. They are also "wholefoods" in the sense that they have not been tampered with before they reach your plate. They are processed or refined as little as possible, if at all. Even canned or frozen beans contain little, if any, of the bad things such as excessive salt, unhealthy fats, or artificial additives and colorings usually found in many "convenience" foods. The versatility of pulses is best demonstrated by the chickpea and the way it is used to such great effect in Middle Eastern dishes. The hugely popular Lebanese dish of hummus (page 17) is simply a purée of chickpeas with lemon juice, garlic, tahini (sesame seed paste), and olive oil. The addition of these simple ingredients transforms this unassuming little legume into a delicious food stuff that can be enjoyed as a dip, a spread, or a sauce. They are also the main ingredient in Falafel (page 22), also a familiar snack often served alongside hummus.

Lentils and dried peas are eaten in India more than anywhere else and are referred to as the "vegetarian's meat". Simply combined with fresh seasonings, such as garlic, ginger, curry leaves, and chile they make incredible curries, such as the Shrimp and Split Yellow Pea Curry (page 116). Although they originated in Asia and North Africa and are still grown there, they are also cultivated in France and Italy. In contrast to the humble dishes of India, the French Puy lentil is highly prized and considered a gourmet ingredient by many. Its nutty bite is works well in salads such as the Lentil and Artichoke Salad with Salsa Verde (page 71).

Grains such as wheat, rice, oats, barley, and corn have been cultivated throughout the world for centuries. They still form a hugely important part of our diet today and come in many guises from whole grains to finely milled flours. They are used in bread and pasta, baked into cakes or cookies, or eaten in a less processed form, as a salad ingredient or breakfast cereal. Why not try one of the new ideas I've included here, such as Barley Risotto with Mushrooms and Goat Cheese (page 120) or Quinoa Choc Chip cookies (page 131).

I hope you enjoy these recipes and use them to create healthy and balanced meals. Don't be afraid to experiment and create your own favorites too!

APPETIZERS

carrot and lentil dip

2 carrots, roughly chopped
1 red onion, chopped
1 garlic clove, chopped
1 teaspoon ground cumin
½ teaspoon ground coriander
½ teaspoon sea salt
3 tablespoons olive oil
½ cup dried red lentils
a handful of cilantro leaves, finely chopped

Serves 6–8

Preheat the oven to 350°F. Put the carrots, onion, garlic, cumin, ground coriander, salt, and 2 tablespoons of the oil in a bowl. Toss and scatter the vegetables on a baking sheet. Cover with foil and cook in the preheated oven for 45 minutes, until the carrots are just tender. Increase the oven temperature to 425°F and cook for a further 10 minutes, until the carrots are golden. Let cool for 10 minutes. Transfer to a food processor and process until chunky. Leave the mixture in the food processor.

Cook the lentils in boiling water for 5 minutes, until just tender. Let sit in the water for 10 minutes then drain well. Add the lentils to the carrot mixture and process until well combined. Transfer to a serving bowl and stir in the remaining oil and the cilantro. Serve with warmed flat breads.

Moroccan fava bean and cumin dip

Here is a simple yet tasty dip that is perfect served with toasted flat breads as part of a sharing plate.

2 cups fresh or frozen fava beans
2 garlic cloves, roughly chopped
½ teaspoon ground cumin
2 tablespoons freshly squeezed lemon juice
¼ cup olive oil
1 tablespoon chopped fresh flat-leaf parsley leaves

Serves 2–4

Bring a large saucepan of lightly salted water to a boil. Add the fava beans and cook for about 5 minutes, until tender. Refresh under cold water and drain well.

Peel the fava beans, discard the tough skins, and put the beans in a food processor with the garlic, cumin, and lemon juice and process until well combined but slightly chunky. Season well with salt and stir in the oil. Transfer to a serving bowl and sprinkle with the parsley. Serve with toasted flat breads.

ful medames

This dish is a popular Egyptian breakfast, served with warmed flat bread, sometimes with sliced hard-cooked egg on the side. It is said that the name of the dish, when translated, means to "bury beans" and comes from a time when the beans were cooked in earthenware pots buried in hot coals.

1⅓ cups dried fava beans (or canned Egyptian brown beans) with skins removed
1 cup dried red lentils
2 teaspoons ground cumin
2 tablespoons freshly squeezed lemon juice
¼ cup olive oil
1 teaspoon sea salt

Serves 6–8

Rinse the fava beans. Cover with water and soak for at least six hours or overnight. Rinse the beans and drain well. Put the beans and lentils in a large saucepan with 3 cups cold water. Bring to a boil, reduce the heat to low, and cover. Cook for 4 hours, barely simmering, until the beans are very soft, thick and mushy. Remove from the heat and stir in the cumin, lemon juice, oil, and salt. Serve with warmed flat breads.

chunky cannellini bean and tuna dip

This recipe uses a little trick of boiling prepared canned beans for a short while to make them a little more tender before they go in the food processor. You can also do this to soften canned chickpeas before blending them to make hummus.

14-oz. can cannellini beans, drained
3-oz. can tuna in olive oil
1 tablespoon olive oil
1 tablespoon small salted capers, well rinsed
1 anchovy fillet (optional)
1 garlic clove, crushed
2 tablespoons chopped fresh flat-leaf parsley
sea salt and freshly ground black pepper

Serves 4–6

Put the cannellini beans in a saucepan of boiling water and cook for 1 minute, just to warm through. Drain well, reserving 2 tablespoons of the cooking water. Put the beans, reserved water, tuna, olive oil, capers, anchovy (if using), and garlic in a food processor and process until chunky.

Stir in the parsley and season to taste with salt and pepper. Transfer to a serving bowl and serve with slices of crusty baguette.

spicy chile bean dip

Shiny, black kidney-shaped black beans are popular in Latin American cooking. They are left whole in this recipe but you could roughly mash after cooking to make them more gooey.

2 cups dried black beans
2 tablespoons olive oil
1 red onion, chopped
4 garlic cloves, chopped
1 red bell pepper, seeded and diced
1 tablespoon ground cumin
2 teaspoons dried Greek oregano
2 teaspoons chili powder
2 x 14-oz. cans chopped tomatoes
a handful of cilantro leaves, chopped
plain Greek-style yogurt or sour cream, to serve
tortilla chips, to serve

Serves 6–8

Put the dried beans in a saucepan with 2 quarts cold water. Bring to a boil, then reduce the heat to a low simmer and cook the beans, uncovered, for about 1½ hours, until just tender and not falling apart. Drain well and set aside.

Heat the oil in a large, heavy-based saucepan set over medium heat. When the oil is hot, add the onion, garlic, and red bell pepper and cook for 8–10 minutes, until softened. Stir in the cumin, oregano, and chili powder and fry for 1 minute, until the spices are aromatic.

Increase the heat to high. Add the tomatoes, beans, and 1 cup cold water and bring to a boil. Reduce the heat to low, partially cover the pan, and cook for 1½–2 hours, adding a little more water from time to time if the mixture catching on the bottom of the pan. Transfer to a serving bowl and serve with the yogurt and cilantro on top and tortilla chips on the side for dipping.

hummus

There are as many variations on spelling this as the day is long. And like any other words translated from Arabic to English, its spelling is inconsistent. In Arabic the word simply means "chickpea" and this ubiquitous dip is more specifically called "hoummus bi tahina" as it is traditionally made with the addition of tahini sesame paste. While there may be many variations on the name, one thing is for sure, this creamy dip is an essential dish at the meze table with tabbouleh, kibbeh, and falafel.

classic:
1 cup dried chickpeas
3 tablespoons tahini
2 garlic cloves
2 tablespoons freshly squeezed lemon juice
4 tablespoons olive oil
1 teaspoon ground cumin
paprika, to sprinkle

smoky paprika:
1 tablespoon Spanish smoked sweet paprika (pimentón dulce)
3 tablespoons tahini
2 garlic cloves, chopped
2 tablespoons freshly squeezed lemon juice
4 tablespoons olive oil
1½ teaspoons sea salt

lemon and cilantro:
3 tablespoons tahini
2 garlic cloves, chopped
2 tablespoons freshly squeezed lemon juice
a small handful of cilantro leaves
4 tablespoons olive oil
1½ teaspoon sea salt

Serves 4–6

Put the chickpeas in a bowl with 4 cups cold water and soak for 6 hours or overnight. Bring a large saucepan of water to a boil. Drain the chickpeas and add to the boiling water. Bring to a boil then reduce the heat to a simmer. Cook, uncovered, for about 1 hour, until very tender. Drain over a bowl, reserving the cooking liquid.

For the Classic Hummus, put the chickpeas and ¾ cup of the hot cooking liquid in a food processor with the tahini, garlic, lemon juice, and cumin and process until smooth. With the motor running, add 3 tablespoons of the oil until smooth and thick. Transfer to a serving plate, making a well in the center. Pour the remaining oil into the well and sprinkle over the paprika.

For the Smoky Paprika Hummus, soak and cook the chickpeas as above. Transfer to a food processor with ¾ cup of the reserved cooking liquid, paprika, tahini, garlic, lemon juice, oil, and salt and process to a smooth and thick paste.

For the Lemon and Cilantro Hummus, soak and cook the chickpeas as above. Transfer to a food processor with ¾ cup of the reserved cooking liquid, tahini, garlic, lemon juice, cilantro, oil, and salt and process to a smooth and thick paste.

Transfer to a serving bowl or spread out on a large serving plate and serve with toasted flat breads.

chickpea pakoras with mango yogurt

14-oz. can chickpeas, drained
1 medium potato, chopped
1 cup frozen peas
¼ cup light olive oil
2 large fresh green chiles, finely chopped
2 scallions, finely chopped
1 teaspoon finely grated fresh ginger
1 teaspoon each of ground turmeric and cumin
a handful of cilantro leaves, finely chopped
3 tablespoons besan (chickpea flour)
1 tablespoon freshly squeezed lemon juice
a generous pinch of sea salt

Mango yogurt:
3 tablespoons smooth mango chutney
¾ cup thick plain yogurt

Makes 24

Cook the chickpeas and potato in a large saucepan of boiling water for 15 minutes, until the potato is tender. Drain well and transfer to a food processor. Process until roughly chopped and chunky. Transfer to a bowl and stir in the peas.

Heat 1 tablespoon of the oil in a skillet set over medium heat. Add the chiles, scallions, and ginger and cook for 2–3 minutes, until softened. Stir in the turmeric and cumin and cook for 1 minute, until aromatic. Add this mixture to the chickpea mixture, along with the cilantro, besan, lemon juice, and salt. Stir to just combine. Use your hands to form the mixture into 24 walnut-size balls, then gently press to flatten each into a pattie.

Heat the remaining oil in a skillet set over medium/high heat. Cook the patties in batches until golden on both sides. Transfer to a plate lined with paper towels. Swirl the mango chutney into the yogurt and serve alongside the pakoras.

chickpea, pumpkin, and cilantro fritters

1 tablespoon vegetable oil
1 small red onion, chopped
1 large fresh green chile, thinly sliced
1 garlic clove, finely chopped
1 teaspoon finely grated fresh ginger
1 teaspoon turmeric
1 teaspoon cumin seeds
1 teaspoon garam masala
1 lb. peeled pumpkin, cut into large pieces
1 cup canned chickpeas, well drained and rinsed
½ cup fresh or frozen peas
2 tablespoons besan (chickpea flour)
a handful of cilantro leaves, roughly chopped
½ teaspoon sea salt
vegetable oil, for deep frying
hot chili dipping sauce, to serve

Makes 24

Heat the oil in a skillet set over high heat and cook the onion, chile, garlic, and ginger for 2–3 minutes, until softened. Stir in the turmeric, cumin, and garam masala and cook for 1 minute, until aromatic. Remove from the heat.

Cook the pumpkin in a large saucepan of boiling water for 10 minutes. Add the chickpeas and peas and cook for a further 2 minutes, until the pumpkin is tender. Drain well and roughly mash with a potato masher, making sure the chickpeas are roughly broken up. Combine in a bowl with the onion and toasted spice mixture, besan, cilantro, and salt.

Fill a heavy-based saucepan one-third full with vegetable oil and heat over medium/high heat. The oil is ready when surface of the oil is shimmering. Using slightly wet hands, form the mixture into walnut-size balls and drop them directly into the hot oil, 5–6 at a time, and cook until golden. Transfer to a plate lined with paper towels. Serve with hot chili sauce for dipping.

dolmades with green lentils, currants, and herbs

Have you ever tried making, and then eating, your own dolmades? These are grape leaves wrapped around a mixture of rice, herbs, and sometimes nuts. Good homemade ones bear little or no resemblance to the canned version, which lack freshness and flavor. This recipe has the addition of lentils as well as rice, sweet currants, pine nuts, and earthy herbs.

8-oz. jar grape leaves

1 tablespoon olive oil

1 small onion, finely chopped

⅔ cup short grain (pudding) rice

¼ cup dried green lentils

½ cup chicken or vegetable stock

2 tablespoons currants

⅓ cup lightly toasted pine nuts

2 tablespoons finely chopped fresh mint

2 tablespoons finely chopped fresh flat-leaf parsley

2 tablespoons finely chopped fresh dill

¼ cup extra virgin olive oil

2 tablespoons freshly squeezed lemon juice

sea salt and freshly ground black pepper

Makes 24

To prepare the grape leaves, separate the leaves and soak in cold water for about 15 minutes. Drain well and pat dry with paper towels.

Heat the 1 tablespoon oil in a small saucepan set over high heat and cook the onion for 2–3 minutes, until softened. Stir in the rice and lentils for 1 minute. Add the stock, stir to combine and to remove any grains stuck to the bottom of the pan. Cover and cook over low heat for 10 minutes. Tip the mixture into a bowl and stir in the currants, pine nuts, mint, parsley, and dill and season well.

Pick out 24 of the largest, least torn grape leaves to use for the dolmades. Use the remaining leaves to line the base of a large, heavy-based saucepan and pour over half of the extra virgin olive oil.

Lay a vine leaf, vein-side down, on a work surface. Put 1 tablespoon of the filling in the center of the leaf and fold the stalk end over, bringing the sides in as you roll to enclose the filling. Do not roll up too firmly, as the rice will expand and cause the leaves to split. Repeat to use all the filling. Pack the dolmades into the saucepan, so they fit snugly in one layer. Pour over the remaining, lemon juice and 2 cups cold water. Gently bring to a boil then reduce heat to low simmer. Cover with an inverted plate and cook over low heat for 45 minutes. Let sit in the pan for a few minutes and when cool enough to handle, remove from the pan and serve.

falafel with minted yogurt

Many recipes using legumes are Middle Eastern in origin, such as falafel, a popular street food. It is a pattie made using dried chickpeas or fava beans or a combination of the two. This recipe does not cook the beans—they are soaked then puréed to a crumbly texture before being combined with the other ingredients.

¾ cup dried fava beans, preferably peeled
1 cup dried chickpeas
1 large onion, chopped
8 garlic cloves, chopped
a small bunch of fresh flat-leaf parsley, chopped
leaves from a bunch of cilantro, chopped
1 tablespoon ground cumin
2 teaspoons ground coriander
¼ teaspoon chili powder
2 teaspoons sea salt
vegetable oil, for shallow frying
flat breads, to serve

Minted yogurt:
1 cup plain Greek-style yogurt
2 garlic cloves, crushed
a handful of fresh mint leaves, finely chopped

Makes about 30

Soak the fava beans in cold water for 24 hours. Soak the chickpeas in cold water for at least 12 hours or overnight. If using unpeeled fava beans you will need to rub the skins off and discard them.

Put the fava beans in a food processor and process until fine and crumbly. Transfer to a large bowl. Do the same with the chickpeas, putting them in the bowl with the fava beans.

Put the onion, garlic, parsley, and cilantro in a food processor and process until well combined. Add this mixture to the beans with the cumin, ground coriander, chili powder, and salt.

Use a large spoon to combine the mixture. Set aside and let sit for 30 minutes.

Put sufficient oil in a skillet to come about 1 inch up the side and heat over low/medium heat. The oil is ready when the surface is shimmering and a pinch of the mixture sizzles on contact with the oil.

Using two dessert spoons, form the mixture into oval patties. Drop directly into the hot oil and cook for 2–3 minutes, until golden and crispy. Transfer to a plate lined with paper towels.

To make the minted yogurt, put the yogurt, garlic, and mint in a bowl and stir well to combine.

Serve the falafel wrapped in flat breads and dressed with the minted yogurt.

salt cod, potato, and butter bean fritters

Salt cod (*bacalao*) is a very full-flavored ingredient and one of the most popular foods of Spain and Portugal. Potatoes make the perfect partner to the cod in these light and crispy fritters and are the traditional ingredient but the addition of butter beans makes them smoother and creamier. Serve with plenty of lemon wedges for squeezing and a little aioli, if liked.

14 oz. salt cod

1 baking potato, peeled and quartered

⅓ cup canned butter beans, drained and well rinsed

2 tablespoons milk

2 tablespoons olive oil

2 garlic cloves, crushed

3½ tablespoons all-purpose flour

¼ teaspoon baking powder

2 eggs, separated

2 scallions, finely chopped

a small handful of fresh flat-leaf parsley leaves, finely chopped

light olive oil, for frying

lemon wedges, to serve

Makes about 36

Soak the salt cod in cold water for 24 hours, changing the water every 6 hours.

Cook the potatoes in boiling water for 15 minutes, until tender. Add the beans and cook for 5 minutes. Drain well and put into a bowl. Mash with the milk and oil until chunky and well combined.

Drain the cod and cut into large chunks. Put into a saucepan and add sufficient water to fully submerge the cod. Bring to a boil and cook for 10–15 minutes, until the water surface is frothy and the fish is tender. Drain and let cool for a few minutes. When cool enough to handle, pick out any bones and flake the flesh with a fork.

Add the cod to the potatoes with the garlic, flour, baking powder, egg yolks, scallions, and parsley. Whisk the egg whites until peaking then fold into the potato mixture until combined.

Fill a heavy-based saucepan one-third full with oil and heat over medium/high heat. The oil is ready when the surface is shimmering and a pinch of the fritter mixture sizzles on contact.

Drop heaping tablespoons of the fritter mixture into the hot oil, without overcrowding the pan, and cook for about 2 minutes, until golden and puffed. Transfer to a plate lined with paper towels.

chicken, white bean, and herb terrine

Summer or winter, a terrine makes a fabulous appetizer or lunch dish. White beans are combined with chicken thigh which in my opinion is much tastier than the breast. This can be made a day or two in advance and in fact benefits from this as flavors develop. Any tangy, chile-spiked chutney or relish will do but fruity mango chutney adds another level of interest.

1 lb. skinless chicken thigh fillet, cut into bite-size pieces

a handful of fresh flat-leaf parsley leaves, finely chopped

1 teaspoon fresh thyme leaves

2 garlic cloves, chopped

1 teaspoon finely grated orange peel

3 tablespoons brandy

½ teaspoon sea salt

½ teaspoon sugar

14-oz. can cannellini or navy beans, drained and well rinsed

1 egg, beaten

12 slices lean bacon

to serve:

mango chutney

toasted bread

a simple green salad

a 9 x 5 inch non-stick loaf pan

a large roasting pan, big enough to take the loaf pan

Serves 6–8

Combine the chicken, parsley, thyme, garlic, orange peel, brandy, salt, and sugar in a bowl. Cover and refrigerate overnight, stirring occasionally.

Preheat the oven to 350°F.

Remove the chicken mixture from the refrigerator and stir in the cannellini beans and beaten egg until well combined.

Lay the bacon slices down the length of the loaf pan, making sure they overlap slightly and hang over the sides. Put the chicken mixture in the pan, firmly pressing down into the pan. Fold the overhanging bacon slices over to enclose the mixture in the pan and cover firmly with a layer of foil, pressing firmly around the edge to seal.

Sit the loaf pan in the larger roasting pan and add enough water to come halfway up the sides of the pan. Cook in the preheated oven for 1½ hours. Allow the terrine to cool in the pan, covered.

Thickly slice and serve with mango chutney, toasted bread, and a simple green salad.

black lentils with lemon juice

This popular lentil dish can be found all over the Middle East from Lebanon to Iraq. Use Indian black lentils (*urad daal*) if you can find them—they are nutty with a chewy texture and very similar to French Puy lentils. You'll find them in Indian grocers or health food stores. If you can't find them substitute Puy. Serve with strips of warm pita bread for dipping.

2 cups black lentils

2 medium potatoes, roughly chopped

2 tablespoons all-purpose flour

3 tablespoons olive oil

4 garlic cloves, chopped

2 shallots, thinly sliced

a small bunch of cilantro, finely chopped

¼ cup freshly squeezed lemon juice

sea salt and freshly ground black pepper

pita bread, to serve

Combine the lentils in a saucepan with 2 cups cold water. Set over high heat, bring to a boil, and cook for 15 minutes. Add the potatoes and cook for a further 15 minutes, until the lentils and potatoes are just tender.

Combine the flour and 2–3 tablespoons cold water in a small bowl to make a smooth paste. Add to the lentils, stirring well to combine and cook for 2 minutes, until the lentil mixture has thickened. Remove from the heat.

Heat the oil in a skillet set over medium heat. Add the garlic and shallots, cook for 1 minute, then add to the lentils along with the cilantro and lemon juice. Season well and serve warm or cold.

lamb kibbeh with garlic sauce

Here, softened bulgur wheat is molded around a lamb mixture to make sausage shapes. This is a Syrian recipe, as is the pungent sauce. The strong garlic flavor will linger on the palate for hours after eating; in a good way!

1½ cups fine bulgur wheat
4 oz. lean ground lamb
1 onion, grated
½ teaspoon allspice
½ teaspoon ground cumin

filling:
1 tablespoon olive oil
1 small onion, finely chopped
2 garlic cloves, chopped
3 oz. lean ground lamb
¼ teaspoon allspice
¼ teaspoon ground cinnamon
2 tablespoons pine nuts, lightly toasted and roughly chopped
a large handful of fresh mint leaves, finely chopped
sea salt and freshly ground black pepper
vegetable oil, for frying

garlic sauce:
6 garlic cloves, peeled
½ teaspoon sea salt
¾ cup real mayonnaise

a baking sheet, lined with parchment paper

Serves 4–6

Put the bulgur in a small heatproof bowl. Pour over enough boiling water to completely cover and leave for 5 minutes. Tip the bulgur into a fine strainer and press to remove as much water as possible. Leave to drain.

Put the bulgur, lamb, onion, allspice, and cumin in a food processor and process to a paste, scraping down the sides of the bowl from time to time. Transfer to a bowl, cover, and refrigerate for at least 1 hour.

For the filling, heat the oil in a skillet set over high heat. Add the onion and garlic and stir-fry for 4–5 minutes, until softened and golden, Add the lamb, allspice, and cinnamon and stir-fry for 4–5 minutes, until the lamb is brown and aromatic. Transfer to a bowl and stir in the pine nuts and mint. Season well and let cool.

Take about 2 tablespoons of the bulgur mixture and roll in slightly wet hands to form an oval, log shape about 2¼ inches long. With wet hands, use your thumb to press an indentation down the center of the log. Fill this with about 2 teaspoons of the lamb filling. Mold around the bulgur mixture to enclose, forming a torpedo shape. Repeat to make 15 in total and put on the prepared baking sheet. Refrigerate for at least 1 hour.

Pour in sufficient oil to come one-third of the way up the side of a large skillet. Set over medium heat. The oil is ready when the surface is shimmering and a pinch of the mixture sizzles on contact with the oil. Add several kibbeh at a time and cook for 2–3 minutes, turning often so they cook to an even golden color all over. Transfer to a plate lined with paper towels.

To make the sauce, chop the garlic and sprinkle the salt over the top. Continue chopping until the garlic forms a paste. Put in a bowl with the mayonnaise and stir well to combine. Serve alongside the kibbeh.

SOUPS

three sisters soup

Referred to as "the three sisters" by native American Indians, beans, corn, and squash are an indelible part of this cuisine.

¼ cup dried butter beans

4 ripe Italian plum tomatoes (such as Roma)

1 large fresh jalapeño chile

4 garlic cloves, unpeeled

2 tablespoons olive oil

1 onion, chopped

2 ears of fresh corn, shucked (about 1 cup kernels)

4 oz. small yellow squash (pattypan or similar), quartered

4 oz. thin green beans, trimmed and halved

2 cups vegetable stock

2 tablespoons freshly squeezed lime juice

a handful of cilantro sprigs, roughly chopped

sea salt

Serves 4

Soak the butter beans in cold water overnight. Drain and put in a large saucepan with sufficient cold water to cover. Bring to a boil, reduce the heat and simmer, uncovered, for 1 hour, until tender. Drain and set aside.

Preheat the oven to 425°F.

Put the tomatoes, chile, and garlic on a baking sheet and cook in the preheated oven for about 10–15 minutes, until the skins darken and begin to blister. Remove the baking sheet from the oven, transfer everything to a clean plastic bag, and seal. When cool enough to handle, peel the tomatoes, chile, and garlic. Discard the skins, and coarsely chop the flesh. Set aside.

Heat the oil in a large saucepan set over medium heat. Add the onion and corn with a pinch of salt and cook for 10 minutes, stirring often until softened. Stir in the tomato mixture, squash, green beans, butter beans, and stock and bring to a boil. Reduce the heat to medium and simmer, uncovered, for 10 minutes, until the green beans are tender. Stir in the lime juice, garnish with a few small sprigs of cilantro, and serve.

creamy curried parsnip and butter bean soup

This is a real winter warmer, perfect for a weekend treat at the end of a cold day. Don't overlook the parsnip, it's a really tasty root veggie and inexpensive too at the right time of year, just when you want to eat it most.

2 tablespoons butter

1 onion, chopped

2 garlic cloves, chopped

2 tablespoons mild curry powder

1 lb. parsnips, chopped

4 cups vegetable stock

14-oz. can butter beans, well drained and rinsed

½ cup light cream

1–2 tablespoons freshly snipped chives

sea salt and freshly ground black pepper

flat breads, to serve

Serves 4

Heat the butter in a large saucepan set over medium heat. When the butter is sizzling, add the onion and garlic with a pinch of salt and cook for 10 minutes, until the onion has softened.

Stir in the curry powder and cook for 1 minute until aromatic. Add the parsnips, stock, and beans and bring to a boil. Reduce the heat and simmer, uncovered, for 30 minutes, until the parsnips and beans are tender.

Remove from the heat and let cool for about 10 minutes. Transfer the mixture in batches to a food processor and process until smooth. Return the soup to a clean saucepan and set over low heat. Stir in the cream and season to taste with salt and pepper. Sprinkle over the chives. Serve with flat breads.

pasta e fagioli

This hearty soup of pasta and beans is a classic from the Puglia region of Italy. In my version of the recipe I like to replace the beans with creamy chickpeas and, if liked, you can add some diced chorizo or pancetta to the pan when you cook off the onions. The pasta shapes traditionally used are orecchiette, meaning "little ears" but any small shape will work just as well.

1¼ cups dried chickpeas
2 tablespoons olive oil
1 onion, finely chopped
2 garlic cloves, finely chopped
a sprig of fresh rosemary
¼ teaspoon dried hot pepper flakes
14-oz. can chopped tomatoes
1 tablespoon tomato paste
6 cups vegetable stock
⅔ cup small pasta shapes such as orecchiette or conchigliette
sea salt and freshly ground black pepper

to serve:
freshly grated Parmesan
extra virgin olive oil

Serves 4

Soak the chickpeas in cold water overnight. Drain and put in a large saucepan with sufficient cold water to cover. Bring to a boil, reduce the heat to medium and cook, uncovered, for 45 minutes, until very tender. Drain and set aside.

Heat the oil in a large, heavy-based saucepan set over medium heat. Add the onion, garlic, rosemary, and hot pepper flakes along with a pinch of salt and cook for 8–10 minutes, stirring often, until the onion has softened.

Increase the heat to high. Stir in the tomatoes, tomato paste, stock, and the chickpeas and bring to a boil. Add the pasta, reduce the heat to a medium simmer, and cook for about 20 minutes, until the pasta is tender. Season to taste with salt and pepper.

Serve sprinkled with Parmesan and drizzled with olive oil.

Moroccan harira

Variations of this soup can be found throughout the Islamic world. In Morocco there are at least a dozen versions but most include lamb, chickpeas, lentils, and spicy cumin. Thick and hearty, this recipe is somewhere between a soup and a stew and can be served as a meal on its own with plenty of crusty bread for dunking. Also, I really don't like using too many pots and pans so this is all done in one pot.

2 tablespoons butter
2 tablespoons olive oil
2 onions, chopped
3 garlic cloves, chopped
2 teaspoons ground cumin
2 teaspoons paprika
1 bay leaf
4 cups beef stock
2 tablespoons tomato paste
14-oz. can chopped tomatoes
1 lb. lamb shoulder meat, cut into bite-size pieces
14-oz. can chickpeas, drained and well rinsed
¼ cup dried brown lentils
leaves from a small bunch of cilantro, roughly chopped
sea salt and freshly ground black pepper
lemon wedges, to serve

Serves 4

Heat the butter and oil in a large, heavy-based saucepan set over medium heat. When the butter is sizzling, add the onion and garlic along with a pinch of salt and cook for 8–10 minutes, stirring often until softened.

Stir in the cumin, paprika, and bay leaf and cook for 1 minute, until aromatic. Add the stock, tomato paste, tomatoes, and lamb and bring to a boil. Reduce the heat to a low simmer, partially cover, and cook for 1 hour. Add the chickpeas and lentils and cook for 1 hour more, until the lamb is very tender and the lentils cooked through. Season to taste with salt and pepper and sprinkle over the cilantro. Serve with the lemon wedges on the side to squeeze into the soup and crusty bread.

Vegetarian option: Reduce the stock quantity by half (and use vegetable stock). Instead of adding the lamb to the pan with the stock, tomato paste, and tomatoes, add the chickpeas and lentils and let it all gently simmer over low heat until the lentils have softened and the soup thickened.

creamy cannellini, leek, and sorrel soup

The sharp, lemon flavor of sorrel is highly prized in France where it is often teamed with dairy and eggs in classic dishes. Here it works nicely with the pleasingly smooth and creamy texture of cannellini beans.

3 tablespoons butter
1 leek, trimmed and sliced
2 garlic cloves, chopped
3 slices bacon, chopped
2 boiling potatoes, diced
4 cups vegetable or chicken stock
14-oz. can cannellini beans, drained and well rinsed
1 bunch sorrel, thinly sliced
½ cup heavy cream
a handful of fresh flat-leaf parsley leaves, finely chopped
sea salt and freshly ground black pepper

Serves 4

Heat the butter in a large saucepan set over medium heat. When the butter is sizzling, add the leek, garlic, and bacon and cook for 10 minutes, until the leek is softened and silky looking and the bacon is golden.

Add the potatoes, stock, and beans and bring to a boil. Reduce the heat to a medium simmer and cook for about 20 minutes, until the potatoes are tender. Stir in the sorrel and cook for a further 5 minutes, until the sorrel has wilted. Stir in the cream and season to taste with salt and pepper. Scatter the parsley over the top and serve.

Vegetarian option: Simply omit the bacon and use vegetable stock for a satisfying meat-free soup.

smoky chorizo and navy bean soup

Here's a short and simple recipe. Small bowls of this can be served up as part of a tapas-style buffet, served with garlicky toasted baguette slices on the side.

2 tablespoons olive oil
6 oz. chorizo sausage
1 red onion, thinly sliced
2 garlic cloves, chopped
½ teaspoon Spanish smoked sweet paprika (pimentón dulce)
14-oz. can chopped tomatoes
2 cups chicken or vegetable stock
14-oz. can navy beans, drained and well rinsed
a handful each of fresh flat-leaf parsley and cilantro leaves, roughly chopped
toasted baguette slices, rubbed with garlic, to serve

Serves 4

Heat the oil in a large saucepan set over high heat. Add the chorizo, onion, and garlic and cook for 5 minutes, until the chorizo has browned and the onion has softened.

Stir in the paprika for 1 minute, until aromatic. Add the tomatoes, stock, and beans and bring to a boil. Reduce the heat to a medium simmer and cook, uncovered, for 10 minutes. Stir in the parsley and cilantro and serve with garlic toasts.

Vegetarian option: Replace the chorizo with 2 cups sliced mushrooms and cook as you would the chorizo. Be sure to use vegetable stock and stir through a few handfuls of baby spinach leaves until wilted for some extra flavor.

spicy pinto bean soup with shredded lettuce and sour cream

A smaller, paler version of the borlotti bean, the pinto has an attractive orange-pink skin with rust-colored specks. It's used extensively in Mexican cuisine, most familiarly in *frijoles refritos* (refried beans). Earthy and savory in flavor, they go well with tomatoes, bell peppers, and cilantro—pretty much all the best-loved flavors of the Americas.

½ cup dried pinto beans
2 tablespoons butter
1 tablespoon olive oil
1 red onion, chopped
2 garlic cloves, chopped
1 red bell pepper, seeded and diced
2 carrots, chopped
2 teaspoons chili powder
2 teaspoons ground cumin
2 bay leaves
6 cups vegetable stock
14-oz. can chopped tomatoes
sea salt

to serve:
1 small iceberg lettuce, finely shredded
sour cream
leaves from a small bunch of cilantro
lime wedges

Serves 4

Soak the beans in cold water overnight. Drain and set aside.

Heat the butter and oil in a large, heavy-based saucepan set over medium heat. Add the onion, garlic, red bell pepper, and carrots along with a pinch of salt. Cook for 10 minutes, until softened. Stir in the chili powder, cumin, and bay leaves and cook for 1 minute, until aromatic.

Increase the heat to high. Add the stock, tomatoes, and beans and bring to a boil. Reduce the heat to a medium simmer and cook, uncovered, for about 45 minutes, until the beans are tender.

Serve topped with shredded lettuce, a dollop of sour cream, and a few cilantro leaves. Offer lime wedges on the side for squeezing.

brown lentil and Swiss chard soup

Using fresh, seasonal ingredients simply prepared is the secret of any good recipe, including this one. Sometimes referred to as continental lentils, the hearty lens-shaped legumes used here do not disintegrate when cooked so make an ideal ingredient for rustic soups and casseroles. For a more substantial soup, add diced chicken breast along with the Swiss chard and let it gently poach in the stock, until just cooked through and tender.

4 cups vegetable or chicken stock

1⅓ cups dried brown lentils

¼ cup olive oil

1 onion, chopped

4 garlic cloves, finely chopped

14 oz. Swiss chard, trimmed and thinly sliced

¼ cup freshly squeezed lemon juice

leaves from a small bunch of cilantro, roughly chopped

sea salt and freshly ground black pepper

Serves 4

Put the stock and lentils in a large saucepan and bring to a boil. Reduce the heat to medium and cook for 1 hour, uncovered, until the lentils are tender. Reduce the heat to low.

Heat the oil in a large skillet set over high heat. Add the onion and garlic along with a pinch of salt. Cook for 4–5 minutes, stirring often, until softened.

Stir in the Swiss chard and stir-fry for 2–3 minutes, until wilted. Add the chard mixture to the lentils and cook over low heat for 10 minutes.

Stir in the lemon juice and cilantro and season to taste with salt and pepper. Serve immediately.

lamb and vegetable soup with split peas and barley

Dried peas come from the field pea not the garden pea, which is eaten fresh. They are available whole or split and the latter have a sweeter flavor which works well here with winter veggies.

⅔ cup dried split yellow peas
2 onions, chopped
1 celery rib, sliced into crescents
2 carrots, chopped
2 small turnips, chopped
⅔ cup pearl barley
1 lb. lamb shoulder meat, cut into chunks
leaves from a small bunch of fresh flat-leaf parsley, finely chopped
2 quarts chicken or vegetable stock
sea salt and freshly ground black pepper
warmed rye or brown bread rolls, to serve

Serves 4

Soak the spilt peas in cold water for 6 hours. Drain and put in a large saucepan with the onions, celery, carrots, turnips, barley, lamb, half of the parsley, and chicken stock.

Bring to a boil, then reduce the heat to a low simmer. Partially cover and cook for 2 hours, stirring often, until the lamb, peas, and barley are very tender. Season to taste with salt and pepper. Sprinkle with the remaining parsley and serve with warmed bread rolls.

Vegetarian option: Turn this recipe into a hearty root vegetable soup by omitting the lamb and adding 1 chopped parsnip, 8 small boiling potatoes, and 10 oz. chopped pumpkin flesh. Cook until the veggies are tender.

pea and ham soup

This old school favorite is a homey, no-nonsense recipe packed with moist and richly flavored ham. I use smoked ham hocks here but the best thing, really, is the leftover hock from a Christmas ham.

2 tablespoons butter

2 onions, finely chopped

1 carrot, roughly chopped

1 celery rib, roughly chopped

1½ cups dried green split peas

a handful of fresh flat-leaf parsley leaves, finely chopped

1 teaspoon fresh thyme leaves

2 smoked ham hocks

2 quarts chicken or vegetable stock

sea salt and freshly ground black pepper

buttered toast, to serve

Serves 4

Heat the butter in a large saucepan set over medium heat. When the butter is sizzling, add the onions, carrot, and celery and cook for 10 minutes, stirring often, until the vegetables have softened.

Stir in the peas, parsley, and thyme for 1 minute. Add the ham hocks and stock. Increase the heat to high and bring to a boil. Reduce the heat to a low simmer, partially cover, and cook for 2 hours, stirring often to prevent the peas from sticking on the bottom of the pan.

Remove the pan from the heat and let cool to room temperature. Remove the ham bones and cut off any fat and skin and discard. Remove the meat and shred. Return the shredded meat to the soup. Return the pan to low heat and cook for 10–15 minutes, just to heat through. Season to taste and serve with buttered toast.

fresh shiitake and barley soup

Fresh shiitake add a satisfying texture to this hearty soup but any variety of fresh mushroom could be used. Dried shiitake are inexpensive and have a long shelf life so make a good pantry staple.

8 dried shiitake mushrooms
1 tablespoon butter
1 tablespoon vegetable oil
4 scallions, thinly sliced
2 garlic cloves, chopped
1 celery rib, chopped
1 carrot, chopped
8 oz. fresh shiitake mushrooms, chopped
2 quarts vegetable stock
1 cup pearl or pot barley

Serves 4

Put the dried mushrooms in a heatproof bowl and pour over 4 cups boiling water. Let soak for 30 minutes. Reserve ½ cup of the soaking liquid. Squeeze out as much liquid as possible from the mushrooms, cut off the stems and discard them. Finely slice the caps and set aside.

Heat the butter and oil in a large saucepan set over medium heat. When the butter is sizzling, add the scallions, garlic, celery, carrot, and fresh mushrooms. Cook for 10 minutes, stirring often, until softened. Add the stock, barley, reserved soaking liquid, and dried mushrooms and bring to a boil. Reduce the heat to a medium simmer and cook for about 40 minutes, until the barley is tender. (Pot barley will require a longer cooking time.) Serve immediately.

barley and fall vegetable soup

This soup has a definite Asian feel to it, with the addition of tamari and sesame oil. But feel free to hold back on the sesame oil and add a sprinkling of finely grated Parmesan on top. The *unami* (savory flavor element of the cheese) complements the tamari.

2 tablespoons butter
1 leek, trimmed and sliced
1 carrot, chopped
8 oz. peeled pumpkin, chopped
8 oz. brown mushrooms, sliced
2 medium potatoes, chopped
2 quarts vegetable stock
1 cup pearl or pot barley
¼ teaspoon ground white pepper
2 tablespoons tamari or dark soy sauce
1 lb. kale, finely shredded
2 scallions, thinly sliced on the angle (optional)
1 teaspoon sesame oil

Serves 4

Heat the butter in a large saucepan set over medium heat. Add the leek and carrot and cook for 10 minutes, stirring often, until the vegetables have softened. Add the pumpkin, mushrooms, potatoes, stock, barley, and pepper and bring to a boil. Reduce the heat to a medium simmer and cook for 45–50 minutes, until the barley is tender. (Pot barley will require a longer cooking time.)

Stir in the tamari and kale and cook for 10 minutes, until the kale is wilted. Serve immediately with a sprinkling of scallions (if using) and drizzled with sesame oil.

SALADS

fava bean, feta, and dill salad

The season for fresh, young fava beans is short. Sometimes called faba, horse, or broad beans, you're likely to find them at farmers' markets in early summer. They need little preparation; just throw them into some boiling water, rinse, drain and add to pastas, risottos, and salads. You can use older frozen or dried beans but you'll need to slip off the tough skins after cooking.

3 cups fresh young fava beans
¼ cup olive oil
1 small red onion, finely chopped
2 garlic cloves, finely chopped
a small bunch of fresh dill, finely chopped
a handful of fresh flat-leaf parsley leaves
a handful of small fresh mint leaves
2 tablespoons freshly squeezed lemon juice
4 oz. feta cheese, roughly crumbled
freshly ground black pepper

Serves 4

Cook the fava beans in a large saucepan of boiling water for 10 minutes. Rinse under cold water and drain well. (If using older fava beans, slip the skins off and discard.)

Heat 1 tablespoon of the oil in a small skillet set over medium heat. Add the onion and garlic and cook for 2–3 minutes, until just softened. Remove from the heat.

Put the fava beans and herbs in a bowl. Whisk together the remaining oil and lemon juice in a small bowl and pour over the salad. Stir to combine. Add the feta, stir again, and season well with black pepper before serving.

pancetta and fava bean salad

This is a wonderfully full-flavored salad or side dish. Pancetta is a fatty bacon that is the Italian equivalent of streaky bacon. It is cured by traditional methods and may be unsmoked or smoked—smoked is preferable for this recipe for an extra level of flavor.

8 slices smoked pancetta
4 cups fresh young broad beans
sea salt and freshly ground black pepper

dressing:
3 tablespoons olive oil
2 teaspoons red wine vinegar
1 teaspoon Dijon mustard
1 garlic clove, crushed
½ teaspoon fresh thyme leaves

Serves 4

To make the dressing, whisk all the ingredients together in a small bowl and set aside.

Preheat the oven to 350°F. Lay the pancetta slices on a baking sheet, without overlapping, and cook in the preheated oven for 5 minutes. Turn the pancetta over and cook for another 5 minutes. Remove from the oven and let cool. When cool enough to handle, roughly tear up the pancetta into smaller pieces and set aside.

Bring a large saucepan of water to a boil and cook the fava beans for 10 minutes, until tender. Drain well and transfer to a bowl of ice water to chill. Drain and transfer to a bowl. Pour in the dressing and add the pancetta pieces. Season to taste with salt and pepper and gently toss to combine. Serve immediately.

slow-cooked lamb salad with fava beans, pomegranate, and fresh mint

Fava beans, fresh or dried, have fed man for millennia. Using them in this recipe results in my favorite type of food to eat; simple, casual, and flavorsome. Lamb shoulder cannot be rushed. When cooked with patience it will melt in your mouth.

2 tablespoons light olive oil
1 tablespoon sea salt
1 tablespoon ground cumin
4 lbs. bone-in lamb shoulder
1 lb. fresh young fava beans
leaves from a bunch of fresh mint
1 pomegranate, seeded
2 tablespoons extra virgin olive oil
2 tablespoons freshly squeezed lemon juice
sea salt and freshly ground black pepper

a rack set over a baking sheet or roasting pan

Serves 4

Preheat the oven to 325°F. Rub the oil then the salt and cumin all over the lamb. Sit the lamb on a rack set over a large baking sheet and cook in the preheated oven for 6 hours. Remove, lightly cover with foil, and let rest for up to 3 hours.

Cook the fava beans in a large saucepan of boiling water for 10 minutes, until just tender. Drain well.

Use a fork or your fingers to shred the lamb off of the bone. Transfer to a bowl and add the fava beans, mint, pomegranate seeds, extra virgin olive oil, and lemon juice. Toss to combine, season to taste with salt and pepper and serve immediately.

spicy three-bean salad

Growing up in Australia, there was a ubiquitous canned "three-bean salad" which was supposed to be eaten with the gloopy sauce it came in. Sorry, but no way! Not when you can make your own delicious and wholesome salad like this one. If you don't have the time to soak the beans overnight, simply replace each of the dried weight with a 14-oz. can of drained and rinsed beans, then toss with the other ingredients.

¼ cup dried kidney beans
¼ cup dried cannellini beans
¼ cup dried fava beans
2 ripe tomatoes
¼ cup olive oil
1 fresh green jalapeño chile, seeded and thinly sliced
1 small red onion, thinly sliced
2 garlic cloves, finely chopped
1 tablespoon white wine vinegar
leaves from a small bunch of cilantro, finely chopped
leaves from a small bunch of fresh flat-leaf parsley, roughly chopped
sea salt and freshly ground black pepper
crusty bread, to serve

Serves 4

Put all of the beans in a large bowl. Cover with cold water and leave to soak for 12 hours.

Drain the beans and discard the water. Cook the beans in a large saucepan of boiling water for 1 hour, until they are tender. Drain and transfer to a large bowl.

Cut the tomatoes in half. Squeeze out and discard as many of the seeds as possible and roughly chop the flesh. Add to the beans.

Combine the oil, chile, onion, and garlic in a small saucepan and set over medium heat. When the ingredients start to sizzle in the oil, remove from the heat and add to the tomatoes and beans. Stir in the vinegar, season to taste with salt and pepper, and stir in the cilantro and parsley. Serve at room temperature or chilled, as preferred, with plenty of crusty bread.

roast chicken and chickpea salad with olives and capers

This is a wonderfully simple summer lunch recipe—one, in fact, that I cook in my café.

⅔ cup dried chickpeas
⅔ cup pitted kalamata olives
3 tablespoons salted capers, well rinsed, drained and roughly chopped
2 small red onions, thinly sliced
2 garlic cloves, finely chopped
4 salted anchovies, finely chopped (optional)
leaves from a large bunch of fresh flat-leaf parsley, finely chopped
¼ cup freshly squeezed lemon juice
¼ cup olive oil
1 cooked chicken (rotisserie is ideal)
1 teaspoon Spanish smoked sweet paprika (pimentón dulce)

Serves 4

Put the chickpeas in a bowl and cover with cold water. Let soak for 6 hours or overnight.

Drain the chickpeas well and cook in a large saucepan of boiling water for about 30 minutes, until tender. Rinse under cold water, drain well, and transfer to a large bowl. Add the olives, capers, onions, garlic, anchovies (if using), parsley, lemon juice, and oil. Stir well to combine.

Remove the meat from the chicken and thinly slice. Add to the bowl containing the other ingredients and stir to combine. Sprinkle the paprika over the top and serve immediately.

Vegetarian option: Omit the chicken and anchovies and double the chickpea quantity. Stir in 16 oz. thinly sliced firm tofu. Let sit at room temperature for about 1 hour, stirring often, so that the tofu is infused with the flavors of the dressing.

heirloom tomato salad with borlotti beans, mozzarella, and summer herbs

When it comes to tomatoes, here in my native Australia we are spoiled by the choice during the summer months, so I like to choose more than one interesting variety, heirloom if possible. Plenty of garden-fresh herbs make the perfect partner for the smooth borlotti beans and creamy mozzarella, making this a delicious salad to enjoy in the warmer months.

½ cup dried borlotti beans

¼ cup extra virgin olive oil

1½ lbs. mixed heirloom tomatoes

1 teaspoon fine sea salt

8 oz. fresh mozzarella cheese (mozzarella di bufala, if available)

a handful of fresh basil leaves, roughly torn

a handful of fresh flat-leaf parsley leaves, roughly chopped

a handful of fresh mint leaves, roughly chopped

sea salt and freshly ground black pepper

crusty bread, to serve

Serves 4

Put the beans in a bowl, cover with cold water, and let soak overnight.

Drain the beans and cook in a large saucepan of boiling water for 40–45 minutes, until tender but not breaking apart. Rinse under cold water, drain well, and put in a bowl. Stir in 1 tablespoon of the olive oil and season well with salt and pepper. Set aside or refrigerate until needed (removing the beans from the refrigerator about 30 minutes before serving).

Thinly slice the larger tomatoes and arrange them on a serving plate. Cut any smaller tomatoes in half and tumble over the tomato slices. Sprinkle the sea salt over the tomatoes and set aside for 15 minutes to allow the flavors to develop.

Roughly tear the mozzarella into bite-size pieces and arrange over the tomatoes. Scatter the herbs over the top and spoon the beans over and around the salad. Drizzle the remaining olive oil over the salad and serve immediately with crusty bread.

Spanish bread salad with chickpeas, chorizo, and baby spinach

Hidden in chorizo are spices that can be enticed out and used to flavor the oil it is cooked in. The warm, spiced pan juices are then tossed with the other ingredients so that the heat gently wilts the spinach. Try substituting chorizo with smoked bacon or pancetta and adding a little extra pimentón.

4 thick slices sourdough bread

3 tablespoons olive oil

2 garlic cloves, peeled and left whole

2 chorizo sausages, thinly sliced

1 red onion, thinly sliced

½ teaspoon Spanish smoked sweet paprika (pimentón dulce)

½ teaspoon dried thyme

14-oz. can chickpeas, rinsed and well drained

8 oz. cherry tomatoes, halved

4 handfuls of baby spinach leaves

2 tablespoons freshly squeezed lemon juice

sea salt and freshly ground black pepper

a ridged stovetop grill pan or heavy cast-iron skillet

Serves 4

Preheat a grill pan over high heat.

Trim the crusts off the bread and discard. Brush both sides of the bread lightly with some of the oil. Add to the preheated pan and cook until golden and slightly charred on both sides. Rub the garlic cloves over the toasted bread and let cool. Tear into large chunks and set aside.

Heat the remaining oil in the pan. Add the chorizo slices and stir-fry for 2–3 minutes, until golden and aromatic. Add the onion, paprika, and thyme and cook for 2–3 minutes, until softened. Transfer to a large bowl and pour in the seasoned oil from the pan. Add the toasted bread, chick peas, tomatoes, spinach, and lemon juice. Season to taste with salt and pepper and toss well to combine. Serve immediately.

Vegetarian option: Smoked tofu makes a good substitute for the chorizo here and tofu or organic vegetarian sausages also work well, if you can find a brand that you like. Simply cook separately, slice, and add to the finished dish.

Mexican taco salad with pinto beans and avocado

The fresh flavors of tomato, avocado, and cilantro form the basis of Mexican cuisine and are combined here in a nutritious salad with little pinto beans and crunchy taco pieces. I find canned pinto beans difficult to source so prefer to soak and cook my own, but if you'd rather use canned beans, kidney beans can be substituted. This is a rather dry salad as it keeps the taco pieces crisp but if you want a dressing, simply add a little good olive oil combined with freshly squeezed lime juice.

¾ cup dried pinto beans

2 firm, ripe avocados

3 ripe tomatoes

⅓ cup pitted black olives, sliced

1 red onion, thinly sliced

leaves from a small bunch of fresh cilantro, roughly chopped

1 crisp lettuce, such as iceberg, shredded

8 stoneground yellow corn taco shells (preferably organic)

Serves 4

Put the beans in a bowl, cover with cold water, and let soak overnight.

Drain the beans and cook in a large saucepan of boiling water for 3–3½ hours, until tender, topping up the water from time to time. Drain well and transfer to a large bowl.

Preheat the oven to 350°F.

Cut the avocados in half and remove the pits. Use a tablespoon to scoop out the flesh in one piece and slice the flesh into wedges. Put it in the bowl with the beans.

Cut the tomatoes in half, squeeze out and discard as many seeds as possible, and thinly slice the flesh. Put in the bowl with the beans and avocados. Add the olives, onion, cilantro, and lettuce and gently toss to combine.

Put the taco shells on a baking sheet and cook in the preheated oven for 8–10 minutes, until crisp. When cool enough to handle, roughly break each taco shell into pieces, and add to the bowl of salad. Gently toss to combine, being careful not to break up the taco pieces and serve immediately.

hot smoked salmon and cannellini bean salad with gremolata

Gremolata is a zesty mixture of parsley, lemon zest, and garlic, sometimes combined with olive oil, that is used in many classic Italian dishes. Here it is used to balance the richness of hot smoked salmon. The addition of buttery cannellini beans make this a satisfying salad.

leaves from a bunch each of fresh flat-leaf parsley and fresh mint, roughly chopped
1 garlic clove, crushed
1 teaspoon finely grated lemon peel
2 tablespoons freshly squeezed lemon juice
¼ cup extra virgin olive oil
14 oz. hot-smoked salmon fillet
14-oz. can cannellini beans, drained and well rinsed
2 small red onions, thinly sliced
1 cucumber, peeled, split lengthwise, seeded, and sliced into crescents
2 handfuls of baby spinach leaves
sea salt and freshly ground black pepper

Serves 4

Combine the parsley, mint, garlic, grated lemon peel, and juice and oil in a small bowl.

Roughly flake the salmon into a large bowl and add the beans, onions, cucumber, and spinach leaves. Season to taste with salt and pepper and toss to combine. Serve immediately with the gremolata on the side as a spooning sauce.

Vegetarian option: Replace the salmon with 14 oz. firm tofu or tempeh (an Indonesian speciality that has a nuttier, more savory flavor than tofu), cut into thin slivers, and add a handful of roughly chopped cilantro leaves for extra flavor.

herbed eggplant, chile, and cannellini bean salad

Eggplant acts like a sponge and soaks up other flavors. Here it is chargrilled and tossed in a spicy herb dressing.

2 large eggplants, trimmed
2 tablespoons light olive oil
14-oz. can cannellini beans, drained and well rinsed
4 handfuls of arugula

herb dressing:
3 tablespoons olive oil
a handful of fresh basil leaves
a handful of fresh flat-leaf parsley leaves
1 tablespoon finely chopped fresh dill
1 large fresh red chile, seeded and finely chopped
2 garlic cloves, chopped
1 tablespoon red wine vinegar

Serves 4

To make the dressing, put the oil, basil, parsley, dill, chile, and garlic in a food processor and process until combined. Stir in the vinegar. Set aside.

Thinly slice the eggplants lengthwise. Brush a stovetop grill pan or large nonstick skillet lightly with some of the oil and heat until hot. Cook the eggplant slices for 2–3 minutes on each side, until golden and crisp. Put the cooked eggplant in a bowl and while it is still warm drizzle over a few teaspoons of the dressing, tossing to coat. Continue until all the eggplant slices and dressing have been used.

Transfer the eggplant to a large bowl. Add the beans, arugula, and remaining oil. Toss to combine and serve immediately.

Greek salad with butter beans

This is a slight twist on a classic Greek salad. Butter beans are a staple of Greek cuisine but are usually served baked in a rich tomato sauce and served as part of a meze. Their delicate flavor works well here with tangy feta and olives. Let sit at room temperature for half an hour before serving.

14 oz. cherry tomatoes, halved

½ cup kalamata olives, halved and pitted

leaves from a small bunch of fresh mint, roughly chopped

leaves from a small bunch of fresh flat-leaf parsley, finely chopped

2 x 14-oz. cans butter beans, drained and well rinsed

3 tablespoons olive oil

2 red onions, thinly sliced

2 garlic cloves, finely chopped

3 tablespoons freshly squeezed lemon juice

6 oz. feta cheese, cut into cubes

sea salt and freshly ground black pepper

bread, to serve

Serves 4

Put the tomatoes, olives, mint, parsley, and beans in a large bowl and toss to combine.

Put the oil in a skillet set over medium heat. Add the onions and garlic. When they start to sizzle in the oil, remove from the heat and pour over the tomato mixture. Stir in the lemon juice and add the feta. Season to taste with salt and pepper and toss well to combine. Serve at room temperature with plenty of crusty bread.

black-eyed pea and red pepper salad with warm halloumi

I have yet to enjoy cold, uncooked halloumi cheese—it really needs to be fried until golden in olive oil before being added to salads or enjoyed as part of a meze. It turns rubbery soon after cooking so serve this salad as quickly as possible after making. If you can find bottled Spanish-style roasted peppers (*pimientos*) in oil, do use these in the salad as they will add extra flavor.

1½ cups dried black-eyed peas (cow peas)
3 fresh plum tomatoes (such as Roma), diced
1 red bell pepper, seeded and diced
leaves from a bunch of cilantro, chopped
¼ cup olive oil
7 oz. halloumi cheese, cut into 1-inch pieces
2 tablespoons freshly squeezed lemon juice
1 tablespoon red wine vinegar
sea salt and freshly ground black pepper

Serves 4

Put the beans in a bowl, cover with cold water, and let soak overnight.

Drain the beans and cook in a large saucepan of boiling water for 1–1½ hours, until tender. Drain and transfer to a large bowl. Add the tomatoes, red bell pepper, cilantro, and half of the oil.

Heat the remaining oil in a nonstick skillet set over high heat. Add the halloumi and cook for 3–4 minutes, turning often, until golden brown all over. Add to the bowl with the tomato mixture and stir in the lemon juice and vinegar. Season to taste and serve immediately.

lentil and artichoke salad with salsa verde

I make this *salsa verde* often and spoon it over rare roast beef, grilled chicken, smoked salmon, or grilled tuna steaks. The capers, anchovies, and pickles have a long shelf life so don't be put off by the long list of ingredients. I have cheated here and used good-quality canned artichokes, which make this very quick and simple to prepare. Try leftovers on bruschetta that has been spread with goat cheese or ricotta.

1 cup Puy lentils
14-oz. can artichokes, drained and quartered

salsa verde:
a handful of fresh mint leaves
a handful of fresh flat-leaf parsley leaves
a handful of fresh basil leaves
2 teaspoons salted capers, rinsed
2 anchovy fillets in oil (optional)
2 garlic cloves
1 medium pickled gherkin
3 tablespoons olive oil
1 tablespoon red wine vinegar
2 teaspoons Dijon mustard

Serves 4

To make the salsa, put all the ingredients in a food processor and process until you have a chunky green sauce. Set aside.

Cook the lentils in a large saucepan of boiling water for about 30 minutes, until tender yet still firm to the bite. Drain well and transfer to a large bowl. Add the artichokes and stir in the salsa. Serve soon after making as the salsa will quickly loose its color.

quinoa tabbouleh

Quinoa (pronounced *keen-wah*) has been grown for thousands of years. The ancient Peruvians called it the "mother of all grains." It is very high in protein and can be used like couscous, rice, or as a substitute for cracked wheat or bulgur.

¾ cup quinoa
3 ripe tomatoes
1 cucumber
4 scallions, thinly sliced
leaves from a large bunch of fresh flat-leaf parsley
leaves from a small bunch of fresh mint

dressing:
¼ cup freshly squeezed lemon juice
1 teaspoon sea salt
¼ cup olive oil

Serves 4

To make the dressing, combine the lemon juice and salt in a small bowl. When the salt has dissolved, whisk in the oil. Set aside.

Put the quinoa in a saucepan and add 2 cups cold water. Set over high heat and bring to a boil. Reduce the heat to a low simmer and cook for about 5 minutes, until the grains are just cooked. Rinse under cold water and drain well. Set aside.

Cut the tomatoes in half, squeeze out as many seeds as possible, and discard. Chop the flesh into small dice. Cut the cucumber in half lengthwise, scoop out the seeds and cut the cucumber into small dice, about the same size as the tomatoes. Combine the quinoa, tomatoes, cucumber, scallions, parsley, mint, and dressing in a bowl and stir until well combined. Serve immediately.

quinoa, corn, and tuna salad

This is a really delicious and healthy salad and one that the kids will love.

¾ cup quinoa
1 tablespoon butter
¼ cup olive oil
2 ears of fresh corn, husked
2 tablespoons freshly snipped chives
leaves from a small bunch of fresh flat-leaf parsley, finely chopped
leaves from a small bunch of cilantro, finely chopped
1 head Boston (soft) lettuce, leaves separated
15-oz. can tuna, drained
1 tablespoon white wine vinegar
sea salt and freshly ground black pepper

Serves 4

Put the quinoa in a saucepan and add 2 cups cold water. Set over high heat and bring to a boil. Reduce the heat to a low simmer and cook for about 5 minutes, until the grains are just cooked through. Rinse under cold water and drain well.

Put the butter and 1 tablespoon of the oil in a nonstick skillet and set over high heat. Cook the ears of corn for 8–10 minutes, turning every 2 minutes, until golden all over. When cool enough to handle, shuck the kernels from the ears and put in a large bowl. Add the quinoa, chives, parsley, cilantro, and lettuce. Roughly flake the tuna and add to the salad. Gently toss to combine.

Whisk the remaining oil and vinegar together in a small bowl. Pour over the salad and toss well. Season to taste with salt and pepper and serve immediately.

Vegetarian option: Replace the tuna with crumbled feta or grated cheddar cheese.

poached chicken and brown rice salad with ginger and lime

I am so glad that brown rice has come out of the back of the kitchen cupboard and is no longer perceived as "hippie food." It has a deliciously nutty and wholesome texture and combined here with Asian flavorings, such as tamari, sesame oil, lime, and ginger, it gets a new lease on life.

1 cup short grain brown rice

1 tablespoon sea salt

2-inch piece of fresh ginger, peeled

2 scallions

a small bunch of cilantro

2 skinless chicken breast fillets

leaves from a small bunch of fresh mint

1 tablespoon sesame oil

¼ cup tamari or dark soy sauce

2 tablespoons freshly squeezed lime juice

1 teaspoon sugar

lime wedges, to serve

Serves 4

Put the rice in a large saucepan with plenty of water. Set over high heat, bring to a boil, then reduce the heat and cook for about 30 minutes, until tender. Rinse under cold water, drain well and put in a bowl.

Put 3 quarts cold water in a saucepan and add the salt. Cut the ginger in half. Thinly slice one half and finely grate the other. Put the sliced ginger in the saucepan with the water and put the grated ginger in a bowl. Roughly chop the scallions (green parts only) and add to the pan. Finely chop the white parts and add to the reserved grated ginger. Cut the stems off the cilantro and add to the water. Roughly chop the cilantro leaves and add these to the rice.

Bring the water to a boil then add the chicken breasts, making sure they are fully submerged. Cover the pan with a tight-fitting lid and remove from the heat. Let the chicken poach undisturbed, for 45 minutes. Remove from the water and let cool to room temperature.

Add the mint leaves to the rice. Add the sesame oil, tamari, lime juice, and sugar to the bowl with the grated ginger and scallion whites and stir to combine.

Thinly slice the chicken and add to the rice mixture. Add the dressing, stir to combine, and serve with lime wedges for squeezing.

spiced pumpkin, spelt, and goat cheese salad with arugula

Spelt is one of the most ancient cultivated wheats—rich in vitamins and minerals and in a readily digestible form, unlike ordinary wheat. Because of its high nutritional value it has recently become more a popular choice. If you can't find pumpkin, butternut squash makes a good substitute here.

⅓ cup whole spelt

14 oz. peeled and seeded pumpkin flesh

¼ cup olive oil

½ teaspoon sea salt

½ teaspoon Spanish smoked sweet paprika (pimentón dulce)

¼ teaspoon dried hot pepper flakes

¼ teaspoon ground allspice

⅓ cup unsalted cashew nuts

1 tablespoon white wine vinegar

4 oz. soft goat cheese

4 handfuls of arugula

freshly ground black pepper

a baking sheet lined with baking parchment

Serves 4

Put the spelt in a large saucepan with plenty of boiling water. Set over high heat, bring back to a boil, and cook for about 30 minutes, until just tender yet still firm to the bite. Drain well.

Preheat the oven to 350°F.

Cut the pumpkin flesh into large bite-size chunks and put in a bowl with half of the oil, salt, paprika, pepper flakes, and allspice. Toss to coat the pumpkin in the spiced oil. Tumble the pumpkin onto the prepared baking sheet and pour over any spiced oil from the bowl. Cook in the preheated oven for about 20 minutes. Remove from the oven, scatter over the cashews, and return to the oven to cook for 8–10 minutes more, until the cashews are golden and the pumpkin tender. Remove from the oven and set aside.

Combine the remaining oil and vinegar in a small bowl. Put the spelt, spiced pumpkin, cashews, goat cheese, and arugula in a large bowl and gently toss to combine, without breaking up the cheese or pumpkin too much. Pour over the dressing and season well with black pepper. Serve immediately.

SIDES

lemon and cardamom basmati rice

The Hindi word "basmati" literally means "the fragrant one", and it is considered to be the prince of rice. This recipe is from Southern India and is typically colorful, light, and zesty.

1½ cups basmati rice
3 cardamom pods
½ teaspoon ground turmeric
2 tablespoons freshly squeezed lemon juice
3 tablespoons rice bran oil
1 tablespoon black mustard seeds
6–8 curry leaves (fresh or dried)
1 tablespoon finely grated fresh ginger
1 tablespoon finely grated lemon peel
leaves from a small bunch of cilantro, finely chopped
sea salt

Serves 4

Put the rice in a strainer and rinse under cold water until the water runs clear. Transfer the rice to a large saucepan, add 3 cups cold water, and set over high heat. Add the cardamom, turmeric, and a pinch of salt to the pan and stir well to combine. Bring to a boil, reduce the heat to a simmer, and cook for about 20 minutes, until the rice is tender. Drain well and transfer to a large bowl. Stir in the lemon juice.

Heat the oil in a small saucepan set over high heat. Add the mustard seeds and cook until they pop. Stir in the curry leaves and ginger and cook for 1 minute. Pour the oil and spices over the rice and stir well to combine. Stir in the grated lemon peel and cilantro just before serving.

tamari brown rice with pumpkin seeds

This is a really wholesome recipe, and a very simple one too. Tamari is used here; it is similar to dark soy sauce in flavor but made without wheat, a common ingredient in the fermentation of soy sauce. It can be used as a substitute for soy in many recipes, such as marinades, dressings, and dipping sauces, and as a general condiment for many Asian-style dishes.

⅓ cup pumpkin seeds (pepitas)
2 tablespoons tamari or dark soy sauce
1 tablespoon sesame oil
½ teaspoon sugar
½ teaspoon sea salt
1⅓ cups long grain brown rice

Serves 4

Dry fry the pumpkin seeds in a small skillet set over low heat, until just golden. Set aside.

Put the tamari, sesame oil, sugar, and salt in a bowl. Stir until the sugar and salt have dissolved.

Fill a large saucepan with water and set over high heat. Bring to a boil and add the rice. Stir a few times, then reduce the heat to a simmer and cook for 30 minutes, until tender.

Drain well and while still warm stir in the tamari mixture until well combined. Sprinkle the toasted pumpkin seeds over the top just before serving.

Southern-style red beans and rice

This dish typifies southern American cooking, particularly that of Louisiana, and is Creole in origin. My recipe is not entirely traditional as it's a dish that can sometimes be stodgy and unappealing, so my version is lighter but still very tasty. I've used kidney beans but smaller South Louisiana red beans could be used if you can find some. This recipe would almost always include leftover pork, ham, or sausage so do add if you have some to hand.

1½ cups dried kidney beans

2 onions

4 cloves

2 sprigs of fresh thyme

1 bay leaf

2 tablespoons rice bran oil

2 garlic cloves, finely chopped

1½ cups jasmine rice

3 cups vegetable stock

a small bunch of cilantro, finely chopped

sea salt and freshly ground black pepper

Serves 4

Soak the beans in cold water overnight. Drain and transfer to a large saucepan.

Peel one of the onions and push the cloves firmly into the flesh. Put the onion in the saucepan with the beans, along with the thyme sprigs and bay leaf. Set over high heat and cover with 2 quarts cold water. Bring to a boil, reduce the heat to a medium simmer, and cook for about 1½–2 hours, topping up with water if necessary, until the beans are tender. Drain well, discarding the onion and herbs.

Finely chop the remaining onion. Heat the oil in a large saucepan set over high heat. Add the onion and garlic and cook for 4–5 minutes, until golden. Add the rice and cook for 1 minute, until glossy and shiny. Add the stock, letting it sizzle and boil. Reduce the heat to a low simmer, cover with a tight-fitting lid, and cook for 15 minutes. Fluff the rice up and stir in the beans and cilantro. Season to taste with salt and pepper. Serve whilst hot.

Moroccan-spiced brown rice with almonds and currants

Here is a deliciously different rice dish with plenty of flavor and texture thanks to the addition of sweet currants and toasted almonds. Serve as a side dish with any roasted meats, grilled chicken, or fish or as part of a cold buffet.

1⅓ cups long grain brown rice
⅓ cup currants
1 cinnamon stick
¼ cup olive oil
2 red onions, thinly sliced
1 teaspoon ground cumin
½ teaspoon sea salt
⅓ cup flaked almonds or shelled unsalted pistachios
2 tablespoons freshly squeezed lemon juice
1 large fresh red chile, seeded and finely chopped

Serves 4

Put the rice, currants, and cinnamon stick in a large saucepan and add 3 cups cold water. Stir to combine and set over high heat. Bring to a boil, reduce the heat to a low simmer, cover with a tight-fitting lid, and cook for 45 minutes, until the rice is tender.

Fluff the rice up with a fork to separate as many grains as possible. Remove from the heat, recover with the lid, and let sit for a further 5 minutes. Discard the cinnamon stick. Tip the rice into a large bowl and let cool.

Heat the oil in a skillet set over high heat. Add the onions, cumin, and salt and cook for 8–10 minutes, until the onions are crisp, golden, and aromatic. Let cool, then stir into the rice.

Dry fry the almonds in a small skillet set over low heat, until just golden. Stir into the rice mixture along with the lemon juice and chile. Serve at room temperature or chilled, as preferred.

Tuscan beans with fresh sage

This recipe is what cooking with legumes is all about—the herbs infuse the water in which the beans are cooked and add plenty of flavor. Simple.

2 cups dried cannellini or
haricot beans
2 sprigs of fresh sage
1 fresh bay leaf
1 head garlic, cloves separated
¼ cup extra virgin olive oil
leaves from a small bunch of fresh
flat-leaf parsley, finely chopped
1 teaspoon sea salt

Serves 4

Soak the beans in water overnight. Drain and put in a large saucepan along with the sage, bay leaf, and garlic cloves. Cover with cold water and set over high heat. Bring to a boil and cook for about 1¼ hours, until the beans are tender. Drain and discard the sage, bay leaf, and garlic. Stir in the oil, parsley, and salt and serve warm.

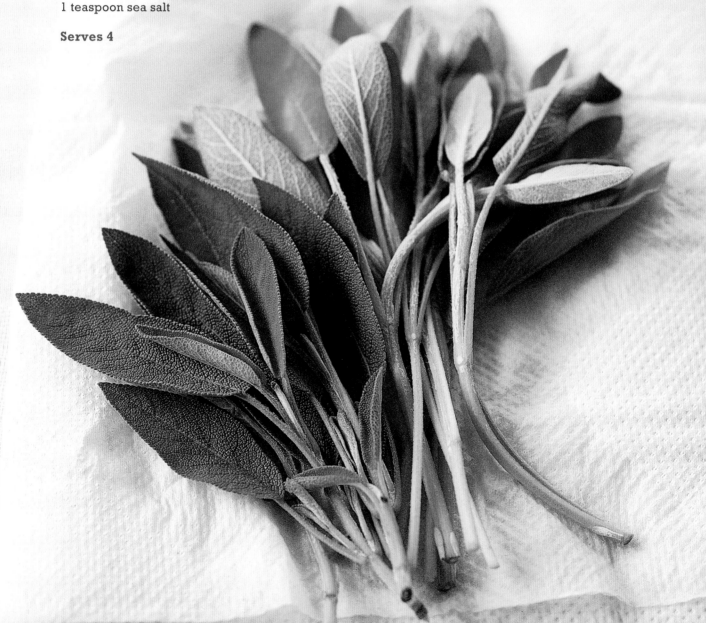

baked inside-out stuffing with wild rice, pine nuts, and raisins

Wild rice is not really rice at all, but an aquatic grass that grows in marshy areas around the Great Lakes and was once a favorite food of the native Americans. As it's somewhat expensive it's often served mixed with long grain rice, as here, to which it adds a deliciously chewy contrast in texture. I refer to this recipe as "inside out" stuffing as although you could use it as you would a conventional stuffing mixture (in a chicken or a rolled loin of pork, for example) cooked this way it can be served as a side dish to both vegetarians and non-veggies. It makes a really great accompaniment to a Christmas roast turkey.

¼ cup wild rice

¼ cup long grain white rice

2 tablespoons butter

2 tablespoons olive oil

1 onion, finely chopped

1 carrot, grated

1 celery rib, finely chopped

2 garlic cloves, finely chopped

½ cup stale bread crumbs

⅔ cup raisins

⅓ cup pine nuts

1 egg, beaten

⅔ cup vegetable stock

2–3 tablespoons extra virgin olive oil

sea salt

a medium baking dish, well buttered

Serves 4

Bring a large saucepan of water to a boil. Add the wild rice and cook for 25 minutes. Add the white rice to the water and cook for a further 10–15 minutes, until both rices are tender. Drain well and transfer to a large bowl.

Preheat the oven to 350°F.

Heat the butter and oil in a large skillet set over medium heat. When the butter is sizzling, add the onion, carrot, celery, garlic, and a pinch of salt and cook for 8–10 minutes, until softened. Add this mixture to the rice along with the bread crumbs, raisins, pine nuts, egg, and stock and mix well to thoroughly combine.

Spoon the mixture into the prepared baking dish and gently press down to compact. Drizzle over the olive oil and cook in the preheated oven for 45 minutes, until golden on top. Serve warm as a side dish.

spicy coconut daal

This recipe is very mushy, almost soup-like, as the lentils soften and absorb the flavors of the spices. If you are lucky enough to find fresh curry leaves, buy heaps and store them in an airtight bag in the fridge.

3 tablespoons rice bran oil
2 onions
2 fresh green chiles, seeded and chopped
1/4 teaspoon ground turmeric
1/2 teaspoon ground cumin
1 1/4 cups dried split red lentils
1 cup coconut milk
1 tomato, chopped
1 teaspoon cumin seeds
1/2 teaspoon black mustard seeds
6–8 curry leaves (preferably fresh but dried are fine)

Serves 4

Heat 1 tablespoon of the oil in a saucepan set over medium heat. Chop one of the onions and add to the pan with the chiles. Cook for 4–5 minutes, until softened. Stir in the turmeric and ground cumin and cook for 1 minute more, until aromatic.

Increase the heat to high. Add the lentils, coconut milk, tomato, and 3 cups water. Bring to a boil, then reduce the heat to a low simmer and cook for 25–30 minutes, stirring often, until the lentils are very soft and mushy. Reduce the heat to very low.

Heat the remaining oil in a small saucepan set over medium heat. Add the cumin and mustard seeds and cook until they start to pop. Finely chop the remaining onion and add to the pan along with the curry leaves. Cook for 2–3 minutes, until the onions are just soft. Stir this mixture into the lentils and cook for 2 minutes. Serve whilst hot.

mujaddarah

This is wonderful comfort food that is eaten all over the Middle Eastern countries, especially in Syria and the Lebanon. It is basically a one-pot dish of spiced rice and lentils, though recipes vary from region to region. You can stir in some garden peas or shelled fava beans for extra color.

1/4 cup olive oil
2 onions, thinly sliced
2 teaspoons cumin seeds
1 1/3 cups dried green lentils
2 bay leaves
3/4 cup basmati rice
leaves from a small bunch of cilantro, roughly chopped
sea salt

Serves 4

Heat the oil in a skillet set over medium heat. Add the onions, cumin, and a generous pinch of salt. Cook for 8–10 minutes, stirring often, until soft and golden. Remove from the heat.

Bring a large saucepan of water to a boil. Add the lentils and bay leaves, reduce the heat to a medium simmer, and cook for 15 minutes. Add the rice, stir, and cook for about 15–20 minutes, until both the lentils and rice are tender. Drain well and transfer to a large bowl. Stir in half of the onion mixture and the cilantro.

Return the pan with the remaining onion mixture to high heat and cook until dark golden and crispy. Spoon the crispy onion mixture over the lentils and serve hot.

Puy lentils with bacon

The tiny, dark blue-green Puy lentil grows in the volcanic soil of the Auvergne region in central France. They are considered to be far superior in taste and texture to other lentil varieties and hold their bead-like shape when cooked. They are perfect for this simple dish, where you want to retain a nutty bite and not cook the lentils down to a soft purée, as you would for Indian daals.

1½ cups Puy lentils
¼ cup olive oil
3 slices bacon, diced
1 onion, finely chopped
2 garlic cloves, crushed
2 tablespoons red wine vinegar
1 tablespoon freshly squeezed lemon juice
a handful of fresh flat-leaf parsley leaves, roughly chopped
2 tablespoons finely chopped fresh mint leaves
a small bunch of chives, snipped
sea salt and freshly ground black pepper

Serves 4

Put the lentils in a saucepan with 4 cups cold water and set over high heat. Bring to a boil, then reduce the heat to a low simmer. Cook for about 25 minutes, until tender yet still firm to the bite. Drain well.

Heat the oil in a large skillet set over medium heat. Add the bacon and cook for about 5 minutes, until golden and crisp. Add the onion and cook for 2–3 minutes, until softened. Stir in the garlic and cook for 1 minute more. Add the cooked lentils, vinegar, lemon juice, parsley, mint, and chives and mix well to combine. Season to taste with salt and pepper and serve warm rather than piping hot.

Iranian rice

This is a simple and novel way of cooking rice. If you have ever cooked potato rösti, this will be dead easy. Precooked rice is cooked in a skillet with butter, forming a large disk shape and frying the rice on the bottom side to a crisp golden brown. Tipped out onto a large plate, it makes for easy serving. Serve with curries, casseroles, and stews.

2¼ cups white long grain rice
1 stick unsalted butter, melted

Serves 4–6

Put the rice in a strainer and rinse under cold water until the water runs clear. Drain well.

Bring a large saucepan of water to a boil. Add the rice and cook for 10 minutes, until the rice is firm to the bite. Drain well and let cool.

Put half of the butter in a large, nonstick skillet and set over high heat. Swirl the pan around to coat it in the melting butter. When the butter is sizzling, add the rice and gently press the rice into the pan using the back of a large metal spoon.

Using the handle of a wooden spoon, make 8–10 small holes or divets in the rice. Melt the remaining butter and pour it into the holes, then pour 1/4 cup water over the rice. Reduce the heat to low, cover the skillet with a tight-fitting lid or with foil and cook for 20–25 minutes. Let the rice cool in the pan for 10 minutes. Shake the pan a couple of times to help remove any stuck on bits.

Take a plate slightly larger than the skillet and sit it on top. Carefully tip the skillet upside-down onto the plate, inverting the rice so that the golden cooked grains are now on top. Serve in slices with curries, casseroles, and stews.

Vietnamese "red" rice

In my hometown of Sydney, Vietnamese restaurants flourish and are well on their way to overtaking Thai as the most popular style of Asian cuisine. You will not see this in all Vietnamese restaurants but whenever I do, I order it. It's a little like a Chinese-style fried rice, but not as substantial; I could eat that as a meal in its own right! The Vietnamese would serve this with a wonderful crispy-skinned chicken. This has inspired me to have this tomato rice as a side to a Sunday roast chicken along with an Asian-style coleslaw.

1⅓ cups white long grain rice
2¾ cups vegetable stock
3 tablespoons safflower oil
3 garlic cloves, crushed
2 tablespoons tomato paste
2 tablespoons butter
1 tablespoon light soy sauce

Serves 4

Put the rice in a strainer and rinse under cold water until the water runs clear. Drain well.

Put the rice and stock in a large saucepan and bring to a boil. As soon as the stock boils, cover with a tight-fitting lid and reduce the heat to low. Simmer for 10 minutes.

Spread the rice out on a large baking sheet and refrigerate for 6 hours, or overnight, turning the rice several times so it dries out. Remove the rice from the refrigerator 30 minutes before cooking.

Heat a wok or large nonstick skillet over high heat. Add the oil, swirling the pan around to coat the base and sides in oil. Add the garlic and cook for a few seconds without burning, just to flavor the oil. Add the rice and stir fry for 2–3 minutes, using a large spoon to break up any large clumps of rice, separating as many grains as possible.

Stir in the tomato paste until it is evenly distributed throughout the rice, turning it red.

Stir in the butter and soy sauce and serve hot.

buttered kasha with corn

Nutty, earthy *kasha* (buckwheat) is a staple food in Eastern Europe, as well as in Russia, where the grain is milled into a speckled grey flour and used to make mini pancakes (*blinis*). Unusually, buckwheat is a complete protein, containing all eight amino acids.

2 tablespoons butter
1 tablespoon safflower oil
2 ears of fresh corn, shucked (about 1 cup kernels)
1 cup kasha (roasted buckwheat groats)
1 egg, beaten
2 cups vegetable stock
a handful of fresh flat-leaf parsley leaves, chopped
a handful of fresh basil leaves, chopped
1 tablespoon finely chopped fresh dill
1 tablespoon finely snipped chives
sea salt and freshly ground black pepper

Serves 4

Heat the butter and oil in a skillet set over medium heat. When the butter is sizzling, add the corn kernels and a pinch of salt to the pan and cook for 2–3 minutes, until the corn is glossy. Set aside.

Put the kasha in a bowl and stir in the beaten egg so that the grains are well coated. Tip the kasha mixture into a nonstick skillet and set over high heat. Cook for 2–3 minutes, stirring constantly, until the kasha looks dry. Add the stock and quickly stir to combine. Reduce the heat to medium/low and cook for 10 minutes, until the stock is absorbed and the kasha is tender. Remove from the heat. Add the corn mixture and herbs and season to taste with salt and pepper. Mix well to combine and serve hot.

spiced buttered couscous

Couscous is made by steaming and drying cracked durum wheat. It is the national dish in Morocco where the traditional way to cook it is to set the grains over a stew and steam it, which requires considerable time and preparation. Luckily for us, precooked couscous is widely available and could not be easier to prepare. Here, this simple accompaniment is taken to another level with the addition of warming spices.

½ teaspoon ground cumin
½ teaspoon sweet paprika
¼ teaspoon ground ginger
¼ teaspoon chili powder
1½ cups couscous
2 tablespoons butter, cut into cubes

Serves 4

Combine the cumin, paprika, ginger, and chili powder in a small skillet and set over medium heat. Shake the pan until the spices are aromatic and starting to smoke, but not burning. Remove from the heat and set aside.

Put the couscous in a heatproof bowl. Add the toasted spices and scatter the cubed butter over the top. Pour in 1½ cups boiling water, quickly stirring a couple of times, then cover the bowl tightly with plastic wrap. Let sit for 10 minutes. Use a fork to fluff up the grains, then cover and let sit for 5 minutes more.

Finally, tip the couscous into a larger bowl and fluff up the grains with your fingertips, separating as many grains as possible for a light-as-air result. Serve warm as an accompaniment.

MAIN DISHES

slow-cooked pork belly with soybeans and miso

In China, soybeans are known as the "meat of the earth" because of their high nutritional value. They are, however, quite bland and need plenty of robust ingredients with distinctive flavors cooking alongside them. The Asian flavors I've used here do the job nicely.

⅔ cups dried soybeans

2¼ lbs. pork belly, in 1 piece

½ cup sake (Japanese rice wine)

1 tablespoon peanut oil

2 teaspoons sesame oil

3 garlic cloves, roughly chopped

4 scallions, white parts only, chopped

5 thin slices fresh ginger

1 cup chicken or vegetable stock

2 tablespoons light soy sauce

2 tablespoons shinshu (light miso)

1 teaspoon sugar

½ teaspoon sea salt

a large, flameproof casserole dish

Serves 4

Soak the soybeans in 3 cups cold water for at least 10 hours or overnight. Drain and transfer to a large saucepan. Add plenty of boiling water and set the pan over medium heat. Cook for 45–50 minutes, until the beans are tender. Drain and set aside.

Cut the pork belly into 8 pieces. Put them in a dish and pour over the sake. Cover with plastic wrap and set aside for 1 hour, turning often. Remove the pork from the sake, reserving the sake.

Put the peanut oil in a flameproof casserole dish and set over high heat. Cook the pork in batches (so as not to overcrowd the pan), for 4–5 minutes, turning often until golden all over. Put the browned pork in a bowl and set aside.

Preheat the oven to 325°F.

Add the sesame oil to the casserole dish. Add the garlic, scallions, and ginger and stir-fry for 1–2 minutes, until aromatic and softened. Add the reserved sake, letting it reach a boil, and cook until the liquid has reduced by half, stirring to remove any stuck-on bits of pork from the bottom of the casserole. Add the stock, soy sauce, shinshu, sugar, and salt and return the pork to the pan, stirring until the shinshu dissolves. Bring to a boil, cover with a tight-fitting lid, transfer to the preheated oven and cook for 2 hours, turning the pork after 1 hour. Stir in the soybeans, cover, and cook for 30 minutes more. Serve hot.

fava bean and pork ragù with tagliatelle

Fava beans have an almost meaty flavor and texture and I guess this is why they have played such an important role in the diet of people in cultures where meat was beyond the means of most people. They often form the basis of rustic country dishes, such as this Italian-influenced recipe.

3 tablespoons butter
1 white onion, chopped
2 garlic cloves, finely chopped
1 carrot, finely chopped
1 celery rib, finely chopped
4 oz. pancetta, finely chopped
14 oz. boneless pork shoulder (Boston butt), cubed
2 teaspoons finely chopped fresh oregano leaves
a pinch of freshly ground nutmeg
½ cup white wine
1 cup beef stock
14-oz. can chopped tomatoes
14-oz. can brown broad beans, well drained and rinsed
14 oz. dried egg tagliatelle
sea salt and freshly ground black pepper
freshly grated Parmesan cheese, to serve

a flameproof casserole dish

Serves 4

Melt the butter in a flameproof casserole dish set over high heat. Add the onion, garlic, carrot, celery, and pancetta and cook for 8–10 minutes, stirring, until the vegetables have softened.

Add the pork, oregano, and nutmeg and stir-fry for 5 minutes, until the pork is lightly browned all over.

Add the wine and let it sizzle for 2 minutes, until it is almost absorbed. Add the stock, tomatoes, and ½ cup cold water and bring to a boil. Reduce the heat to a low simmer, partially cover, and cook for 1½ hours, until the pork is very tender.

Stir in the beans. Using a potato masher, mash the ingredients in the pan, so the pork breaks up and some of the beans are smashed. Season to taste with salt and pepper and let cook over low heat while you cook the pasta.

Cook the tagliatelle according to the package directions and drain well. Tip the pasta into the ragù and toss well to combine. Serve immediately with grated Parmesan for sprinkling.

Vegetarian option: Omit the pancetta and pork shoulder and adjust the cooking time accordingly. Keep the quantity of fava beans the same and add a bay leaf and a sprig of fresh thyme for flavor. Use vegetable stock in place of the beef stock.

pork sausage, fennel, and navy bean stew

My local butcher supplies pork sausages flavored with fennel seeds. This is a very Sicilian idea and they are so good! Other gourmet flavored sausages, such as lamb and rosemary, would be tasty in this recipe too. Navy beans are small, white oval beans that become very tender when cooked, but cannellini beans would work just as well if that's what you have to hand. This is delicious served with soft polenta, mashed potatoes, or crusty bread—basically something to mop up the delicious sauce.

2 tablespoons olive oil
12 small pork sausages
1 onion, chopped
1 fennel bulb, chopped
2 garlic cloves, chopped
½ teaspoon fennel seeds
14-oz. can navy beans, well drained and rinsed
14-oz. can chopped tomatoes
2 teaspoons brown sugar
sea salt and freshly ground black pepper
soft polenta or mashed potatoes, to serve

Serves 4

Heat the oil in a large, heavy-based skillet set over medium heat. Add half of the sausages to the pan and cook for 4–5 minutes, turning often, until well browned all over. Remove from the pan and repeat with the remaining sausages.

Add the onion, fennel, garlic, and fennel seeds to the pan and stir-fry for 5 minutes, until the fennel is softened and golden.

Add the beans, tomatoes, and sugar to the pan and stir to combine. Return the sausages to the pan and bring to a boil. Reduce the heat to a low simmer and cook for 10–15 minutes. Season to taste with salt and pepper and serve with the side dish of your choice.

Vegetarian option: Try using herbed vegetarian sausages and cook exactly as you would the pork ones. I would also be tempted to add a bit of spicy heat, such as a good sprinkling of dried hot pepper flakes or a finely chopped fresh red chile with the onions.

smoky bean and lamb casserole

Navy beans feature in many casseroles from Spain, Portugal, and South America and are the beans most commonly used to make canned baked beans. The beans cook and soften in the pot in this recipe and are infused with the herbs and seasonings with delicious results. The addition of plenty of Spanish smoked sweet paprika (pimentón dulce) is what gives this dish its tantalizingly smoky flavor as well as a deep red sauce.

2 tablespoons olive oil

1 lb. lamb shoulder meat, cut into 2-inch pieces

2 tablespoons butter

2 onions, finely chopped

3 garlic cloves, roughly chopped

1 bay leaf

1 tablespoon fresh thyme leaves

1 tablespoon Spanish smoked paprika (pimentón dulce)

1 cup dried navy beans

2 x 14-oz. cans chopped tomatoes

2 tablespoons tomato paste

leaves from a small bunch of fresh flat-leaf parsley, roughly chopped

sea salt and freshly ground black pepper

lemon wedges, to serve

a large flameproof casserole dish

Serves 4

Heat the oil in a large, flameproof casserole dish set over high heat. Add the lamb and cook for about 5 minutes, turning often, so the pieces are evenly browned all over. Remove from the pan and pour off all but about 1 tablespoon of the oil.

Add the butter to the casserole dish. When the butter is sizzling, add the onions, garlic, bay leaf, and thyme leaves and stir-fry for 2–3 minutes, until the onion has softened and the herbs are aromatic.

Stir in the paprika and cook for 1 minute. Stir in the beans, tomatoes, and tomato paste. Return the lamb to the casserole dish and bring to a boil.

Reduce the heat to low, cover, and cook at a low simmer for 2 hours, stirring occasionally, until the lamb and beans are very tender. Season to taste with salt and pepper and stir in the parsley. Serve with lemon wedges for squeezing.

Vegetarian option: Turn this into a simple bean casserole by omitting the lamb and adding a 14-oz. can drained chickpeas or brown lentils. Reduce the cooking time to 1 hour.

slow-cooked lamb shanks with lentils

This recipe is simply a few of my favorite ingredients thrown together in a pot and the alchemy of cooking does its magic. Make this once and you may be hooked. For a lighter dish, try chicken instead of lamb; choose some lovely Maryland cuts (thigh and drumstick), pan-sear until the skin is golden, then proceed with the recipe from there. Serve this with plenty of mashed potatoes and green beans.

½ cup dried green lentils
4 oz. pancetta or country ham, chopped
2 garlic cloves, chopped
14-oz. can chopped tomatoes
2 cups chicken stock
1 cup red wine
4 trimmed lamb shanks
a handful of fresh flat-leaf parsley leaves, roughly chopped
sea salt and freshly ground black pepper

a large casserole dish or other lidded baking dish

Serves 4

Preheat the oven to 325°F.

Put the lentils, pancetta, garlic, tomatoes, stock, and wine in a large casserole dish and season well with salt and pepper. Stir well to combine. Add the lamb shanks and cover with a tight-fitting lid.

Cook in the preheated oven for 1½ hours. Remove the casserole dish from the oven and turn the lamb shanks over. Re-cover, return to the oven and cook for 1 hour more, until the lamb is very tender. Stir in the parsley. Serve one shank per person with a generous portion of the lentils.

Hungarian goulash with fava beans

While there are many variations of this classic Hungarian dish there is one ingredient that defines goulash: paprika. This recipe not only has plenty of paprika, but the novel addition of fava beans. Their earthy texture goes hand in hand with the warming spices and makes a very tasty dish. Serve with plain boiled rice.

¼ cup light olive oil

4 oz. pancetta, finely diced

2 onions, finely chopped

2 garlic cloves, finely chopped

1 red bell pepper, seeded and finely diced

2 carrots, finely diced

1 lb. beef stewing meat, cubed

2 tablespoons sweet paprika (preferably Hungarian)

¼ teaspoon caraway seeds

1 tablespoon tomato paste

4 cups chicken or vegetable stock

14-oz. can fava beans, drained and well rinsed

a handful of fresh flat-leaf parsley leaves, roughly chopped

sea salt and freshly ground black pepper

boiled rice, to serve

a large, flameproof casserole dish

Serves 4

Heat 1 tablespoon of the oil in a large, flameproof casserole dish set over high heat. Add the pancetta and cook for 5 minutes, stirring often, until golden. Remove from the pan and set aside.

Reduce the heat to medium. Add 1 tablespoon of the oil to the casserole dish, then add the onions and garlic. Cook for 5 minutes, until softened. Add the red bell pepper and carrots and cook for 8–10 minutes, until all the vegetables are softened and golden. Remove from the casserole dish.

Increase the heat to high. Add 1 further tablespoon of oil to the casserole dish. Add half of the beef and cook for 4–5 minutes, stirring often, until well browned. Remove from the casserole. Add the remaining oil and beef and repeat.

Add the paprika and caraway seeds to the casserole dish and stir-fry for 1 minute, until aromatic. Add the tomato paste and stock and stir. Return all the ingredients to the casserole dish and bring to a boil. Reduce the heat to a low simmer and cook for 1½ hours, until the beef is very tender. Season to taste with salt and pepper. Stir in the beans and parsley and cook for 10 minutes to warm the beans through. Serve with plain boiled rice.

Vegetarian option: Omit the pancetta and beef and double the quantity of fava beans. Cook the vegetables and make the sauce with the spices, tomato paste, and vegetable stock as above, but reduce the simmering time to 20 minutes. Add the beans and parsley and heat before serving.

"real" chili con carne

Chili con carne can be whipped up in no time using ground beef but the result is nothing like this. Chuck or stewing steak is a cut I use often as it cooks down to a beautiful tenderness (a texture nothing like ground beef) and absorbs flavorings well. Robust kidney or pinto beans are used in Mexican dishes as white beans, so popular in Italian and French cuisine, would be overwhelmed by all these heady spices.

2 tablespoons olive oil
1 red onion, chopped
2 garlic cloves, roughly chopped
1 teaspoon chili powder
1 teaspoon ground cumin
½ teaspoon ground cinnamon
2 teaspoons dried oregano
1 lb. boneless beef chuck, cut into
1½-inch pieces
1 cup beer
2 tablespoons chipotles in adobo
14-oz. can kidney or pinto beans, drained
and well rinsed
boiled rice, to serve

Serves 4

Heat the oil in a heavy-based skillet set over medium heat. Add the onion and garlic and cook for 4–5 minutes, until golden. Add the chili powder, cumin, cinnamon, and oregano and cook for 1 minute, until aromatic. Add the beef and stir-fry for 5 minutes until the beef is browned.

Add the beer, 1 cup cold water, chipotles, and beans. Bring to a boil, then reduce the heat to a low simmer. Cook for 1½ hours, stirring occasionally, until the beef is very tender and the sauce has thickened. Serve with plain boiled rice.

smoky baked beans

I make these delicious beans in my café where I spoon some of the mixture into individual ovenproof dishes, crack an egg in the center and bake in a hot oven until the egg is just set—the perfect brunch dish. Date molasses are a Lebanese speciality, available from gourmet suppliers and worth seeking out for this dish alone.

1 smoked ham hock
1 onion, finely chopped
¼ cup date molasses plus 1 tablespoon,
or the same quantity of ordinary molasses
1 tablespoon English mustard powder
2 teaspoons cider vinegar
2 cups dried navy beans
½ teaspoon sea salt
sea salt and freshly ground black pepper

a large casserole dish

Serves 4

Preheat the oven to 300°F.

Put the ham hock, onion, ¼ cup molasses, mustard powder, vinegar, dried beans, and salt in a large casserole. Add 2 quarts cold water, stir to combine and cover with a tight-fitting lid.

Cook in the preheated oven for 4 hours, stirring after 2 hours. Remove the lid and cook for another 1½–2 hours until the meat is falling off the bone and the beans are dark and tender. Remove the bone, shred any meat that remains on it into the beans, and discard. Season to taste with plenty of salt and pepper.

Serve at room temperature as a side dish or as a meal on its own, with plenty of bread to soak up the sauce.

white fish, soybean, and baby carrot hot pot

If you happen to live in a city which has a Chinatown or even an Asian speciality food store, do look out for Chinese earthenware pots (sand pots). They are an inexpensive item and make for addictive culinary experimentation! Made from clay and glazed inside, they can be used on both stovetop and in the oven, just like a conventional casserole dish, and are perfect for recipes such as this one.

1¾ lb. skinless white fish fillet, cut into bite-size pieces

½ cup all-purpose flour

2 tablespoons vegetable oil

2 teaspoons sesame oil

4 garlic cloves, roughly chopped

2 scallions, white and green parts, thinly sliced on the angle

1 tablespoon grated fresh ginger

8 baby carrots

2 cups fish or vegetable stock

1 tablespoon Thai fish sauce

14-oz. soybeans, well rinsed and drained

leaves from a small bunch of cilantro, chopped

a large flameproof casserole dish

Serves 4

Put the fish pieces in a strainer with the flour. Toss to coat the fish in the flour and set aside.

Heat both the oils in a large, flameproof casserole dish set over high heat. Add the fish pieces in batches, cooking for just 1 minute on each side, until golden. Transfer the fish to a plate as you go.

Add the garlic, scallion whites, and ginger to the casserole dish and stir-fry for 2 minutes, scrapping the base to remove any stuck-on bits. Add the carrots, stock, fish sauce, and soybeans. Increase the heat and bring to a boil. Cook for 10 minutes, until the liquid has slightly reduced.

Add the fish pieces and gently stir. Reduce the heat to a low simmer and cook for 5 minutes, until the fish is opaque and cooked through.

Stir in half of the cilantro and scatter the remaining cilantro and scallion greens over the top. Serve immediately.

Vegetarian option: Replace the fish with about 7 oz. peeled, seeded, and chopped butternut squash and 1 cup sliced mushrooms, shiitake if available. Increase the cooking time by 5–10 minutes and cook until the squash is just tender. Use vegetable stock and omit the fish sauce.

chickpea and fresh spinach curry

I am a fan of good quality curry pastes but still feel the need to add my own individual, fresh touch when cooking with them. I usually cook off some onion, garlic, and ginger and may add fresh or dried curry leaves and a couple of large red or green chiles, split lengthwise. Chickpeas are popular in India and work brilliantly here in this spicy curry.

1 white onion, roughly chopped

2 garlic cloves, sliced

1 teaspoon chopped fresh ginger

1 tablespoon light olive oil

2 tablespoons mild curry paste

14-oz. can chopped tomatoes

14-oz. can chickpeas, well drained and rinsed

1 lb. fresh spinach, stalks removed and leaves chopped

a handful of cilantro leaves, roughly chopped

Indian naan or roti bread, to serve

Serves 4

Put the onion, garlic, and ginger in a food processor and process until finely chopped. Heat the oil in a skillet set over high heat. Add the onion mixture and cook for 4–5 minutes, stirring often, until golden. Add the curry paste and stir-fry for just 2 minutes, until aromatic.

Stir in the tomatoes, 1 cup cold water, and the chickpeas. Bring to a boil, then reduce the heat to a medium simmer and cook, uncovered, for 10 minutes. Stir in the spinach and cook just until it is wilted.

Stir in the cilantro and serve with the bread of your choice.

shrimp and yellow split pea curry

In the recipe on the previous page I cheat a little and use a prepared curry paste, but a basic curry is easy to make from a few pantry spices and a handful of fresh seasonings. The split peas used here cook down to a mushy consistency, thickening the sauce nicely.

1 large onion, roughly chopped

3 garlic cloves, chopped

2-inch piece of fresh ginger, peeled and chopped

2 large fresh red chiles, seeded and chopped

1 tablespoon vegetable oil

1 lb. jumbo shrimp, peeled and deveined

6–8 curry leaves (dried or fresh)

½ teaspoon ground cumin

½ teaspoon ground turmeric

4 ripe tomatoes, roughly chopped

¼ cup dried yellow split peas

leaves from a small bunch of cilantro, roughly chopped

sea salt and freshly ground black pepper

cooked basmati rice, to serve

Serves 4

Put the onion, garlic, ginger, and chiles in a food processor and process to a paste.

Heat the oil in a large skillet set over high heat. Add the shrimp and cook for just 2 minutes on each side, until pink. Remove from the pan and set aside.

Add the onion mixture to the pan and stir-fry for 5 minutes, until starting to turn golden. Add the curry leaves and cook for 1 minute. Stir in the cumin and turmeric and cook for 1 minute more, until aromatic.

Add the tomatoes, ½ cup cold water, and the split peas. Let the mixture sizzle and boil for 1 minute, then reduce the heat to a low simmer. Cook for 25–30 minutes, until the split peas are just tender and the mixture has thickened. Return the cooked shrimp to the pan and add the cilantro. Cook for 2 minutes, until the shrimp are heated through. Season well with salt and pepper and serve with basmati rice.

Vegetarian option: Dice about 14 oz. paneer (Indian cheese) and fry in a nonstick skillet set over medium heat. Substitute for the shrimp, following the recipe as above.

mung bean and vegetable curry

Mung beans are pretty olive-colored beans native to India and one of the most popular beans for sprouting. Once split and hulled they are yellow, have a slightly sweet flavor and become butter-soft with cooking. They are traditionally used in the Indian curry *moong dhal*, which is flavored with ground coriander, cumin, turmeric, and hot cayenne pepper. I've added carrots to my recipe but you could add chopped pumpkin or butternut squash, baby new potatoes, or cubes of pan-fried eggplant.

1 cup dried split mung beans

2 tablespoons vegetable oil

1 onion, finely chopped

2 teaspoons finely grated fresh ginger

2 garlic cloves, finely chopped

2 fresh green chiles, seeded and finely chopped

8 curry leaves (dried or fresh)

¼ teaspoon ground turmeric

1 teaspoon ground cumin

2 carrots, sliced

14-oz. can chopped tomatoes

2 handfuls fresh spinach leaves, stalks removed and leaves chopped

leaves from a small bunch of cilantro, roughly chopped

sea salt and freshly ground black pepper

Indian naan or roti bread, to serve

Serves 4

Put the mung beans in a large saucepan and add 1 quart water. Bring to a boil, reduce the heat to a low simmer, and cook for 20 minutes. Drain well and set aside.

Heat the oil in a heavy-based saucepan set over high heat. Add the onion, ginger, garlic, chiles, and curry leaves. Cook for 2–3 minutes, stirring often, until the mixture is aromatic. Stir in the turmeric and cumin and cook for 1 minute more.

Add the carrot, tomatoes, mung beans, and ½ cup water and bring to a boil. Reduce the heat to a medium simmer and cook for 15 minutes, until the carrots are tender and the mung beans are soft and breaking up. Stir in the spinach and cilantro and cook for a couple of minutes, until the spinach has wilted. Season to taste with salt and pepper and serve with the bread of your choice.

barley risotto with mushrooms and goat cheese

Barley makes for an interesting substitute for rice in a risotto. It has a nutty and sweet flavor which works well here with both the mushrooms and the red wine and is offset by the creamy tang of goat cheese.

1 oz. dried porcini mushrooms

4 cups vegetable stock

¼ cup red wine

3 tablespoons butter

1 tablespoon olive oil

1 leek, trimmed and thinly sliced

2 garlic cloves, chopped

1⅔ cups pearl barley

14 oz. fresh brown mushrooms, sliced

2 oz. soft goat cheese

a small handful of fresh flat-leaf parsley leaves, finely chopped

sea salt and freshly ground black pepper

Serves 4

Put the dried mushrooms in a heatproof bowl and cover with ½ cup boiling water. Let soak for 20 minutes. Drain the mushrooms and reserve the soaking liquid. Roughly chop the mushrooms and set aside.

Combine the stock, red wine, and reserved mushroom soaking liquid in a saucepan set over low heat.

Heat half of the butter and the oil in a heavy-based saucepan set over medium heat. Add the leek and garlic and cook for about 4–5 minutes, until the leek has softened. Stir in the barley and cook for 1 minute, until shiny and glossy.

Stir in the fresh and dried mushrooms and cook for 2–3 minutes, until the mushrooms have wilted.

Add about ½ cup of the hot stock mixture to the barley and stir constantly, until almost all the liquid has been absorbed. (This will take a little longer than cooking with risotto rice.) Continue adding the liquid a little at a time and stirring for about 45 minutes, until all the liquid has been added and the barley is tender.

Stir in the goat cheese and remaining butter, until the cheese has melted. Season to taste with salt and pepper and sprinkle over the parsley. Serve immediately.

simple tomato and basil risotto

It's hard to beat a simple risotto made with fresh seasonal ingredients. Here summer-ripe tomatoes and sweet, liquoricy basil are stirred into buttery semi-cooked rice; the rice should be a little softened around the edges but still firm to the bite.

3 fresh plum tomatoes
4 cups vegetable stock
¼ cup dry vermouth
2 tablespoons butter
2 tablespoons olive oil
2 garlic cloves, chopped
1 large trimmed leek, sliced
1½ cups Arborio rice
a large handful of fresh basil leaves, roughly torn
½ cup finely grated Parmesan cheese
extra virgin olive oil, to drizzle

Serves 4

Cut the tomatoes in half and squeeze out and discard as many seeds as possible. Finely dice the flesh and set aside.

Put the stock and vermouth in a medium saucepan set over low heat. Put half of the butter and the oil in a heavy-based saucepan and set over medium heat. Add the garlic and leek and cook for 4–5 minutes, until softened. Add the rice and cook for 1 minute, until shiny and glossy.

Add about ¼ cup of the hot stock mixture to the rice and stir constantly, until almost all of the liquid has been absorbed. Add another ¼ cup to the pan, stirring until almost all the liquid has been absorbed. Continue adding the stock mixture a little at a time and stirring, until all the stock has been used and the rice is just tender.

Stir in the tomatoes, basil, Parmesan, and remaining butter until well combined. Drizzle with olive oil and serve immediately.

Chinese Hainan chicken rice

This is actually a rather old-fashioned way to cook chicken. During the Australian summers of my childhood, a big pot of poached chicken on the stovetop was a familiar sight. It would be shredded and used in salads and sandwiches or stirred through soups. But we never had chicken poached with these wonderful Asian flavorings, all now readily available.

a 3½-lb. chicken
a bunch of scallions
8 garlic cloves, lightly smashed
4-inch piece of fresh ginger, peeled and thinly sliced
3 tablespoons sea salt
1⅓ cups jasmine rice
a small bunch of cilantro
ground white pepper
sliced tomato and cucumber, to serve

ginger sauce:
¼ cup light soy sauce
½ teaspoon sugar
8 scallions, thinly sliced on the angle
2-inch piece of fresh ginger, peeled and finely grated
1 teaspoon sesame oil
2 tablespoons peanut oil

Serves 4

To make the ginger sauce, put the soy sauce, sugar, scallions, and ginger in a small heatproof bowl and stir to combine. Combine the sesame and peanut oils in a small saucepan set over high heat. When the oil is smoking hot, pour it over the scallion mixture, stir and set aside.

Trim any excess fat from around the cavity of the chicken. Wash and pat dry.

Put 4 quarts cold water in a large saucepan. Add the scallions, garlic, ginger, and salt and bring to a boil. Reduce the heat to a medium simmer and cook for 30 minutes. Reduce the heat to low and put the chicken in the water, breast-side down, making sure it is fully submerged. Let cook for 15 minutes, then cover with a tight-fitting lid and remove the pan from the heat. Leave to poach for 3 hours. Use tongs to carefully remove the chicken from the pan without tearing the skin. Transfer to a large bowl, cover, and reserve the stock.

Put the rice in a strainer and rinse under cold water until the water runs clear. Combine the rice and 2¾ cups of the reserved stock in a saucepan set over high heat and bring to a boil. When the stock boils, cover with a tight-fitting lid, reduce the heat to low and cook for 10 minutes.

Cut the chicken into 12 pieces. For each serving, put 3 pieces of chicken on a serving plate with the rice on the side. Arrange the tomato and cucumber slices on the plate. Sprinkle over the cilantro and pepper and serve with the ginger sauce in a small bowl on the side.

combination fried rice

I prefer to eat Chinese stir-fries with plain steamed or boiled rice and save this tasty rice dish for special occasions, as it really is a meal on its own. I have kept the ingredients list fairly basic—most of us will have some rice in the kitchen cupboard, so feel free to use whatever you have. You could substitute the bacon for ham and if you happen to live near an Asian speciality food shop, you could add some thinly sliced Chinese sausage or barbecue pork.

⅓ cup peanut oil

4 eggs, beaten

16 raw jumbo shrimp, peeled and deveined

2 garlic cloves, finely chopped

1 tablespoon grated fresh ginger

1 onion, thinly sliced

2 bacon slices, chopped

1 cup fresh beansprouts

1 teaspoon white sugar

6 cups cooked white or brown long grain rice

4 shallots, thinly sliced

1 tablespoon oyster sauce

1–2 tablespoons light soy sauce

½ teaspoon sesame oil

¼ teaspoon ground white pepper

Serves 4

Heat half of the oil in a wok or very large nonstick skillet set over high heat, carefully swirling the wok around to coat the sides in the oil. When smoking hot, add the beaten eggs. Let the eggs sizzle in the oil. When puffed around the edges, use a large wooden spoon to slowly stir the eggs until they are just set. Tip the eggs onto a chopping board. Let cool and roughly chop.

Add the remaining oil to the wok and heat. When smoking hot add the shrimp and stir-fry for 2–3 minutes, until pink. Remove from the wok, leaving the oil in the wok to reheat.

Add the garlic, ginger, onion, and bacon to the wok and stir-fry for 2–3 minutes, until the onion is golden and the bacon starting to crisp. Add the beansprouts and sugar and stir-fry for just a few seconds to combine and until the beansprouts have wilted.

Add the rice, shallots, oyster sauce, soy sauce, sesame oil, and pepper to the wok and stir-fry for 2–3 minutes, until well combined and the rice has heated through. Add the eggs and shrimp to the wok, stir well to combine and serve immediately.

SWEET THINGS & BAKING

Anzac cookies

In Australia and New Zealand these are known as Anzac biscuits and are a popular home-baked treat. I've used unprocessed whole oats here, as they have the nutritious bran and germ remaining intact. Baking them for a little less time will result in a chewy texture and cooking them for a little longer will result in a crisp cookie.

¾ cup unsweetened desiccated coconut
1 cup organic whole oats
1 cup all-purpose flour
1 cup plus 2 tablespoons natural cane sugar
1 stick unsalted butter
1 tablespoon honey
1 teaspoon baking soda

1–2 baking sheets lined with baking parchment

Makes about 30 cookies

Preheat the oven to 350°F.

Put the coconut, oats, flour, and sugar in a bowl and stir to combine. Make a well in the center.

Put the butter, honey, and 2 tablespoons cold water in a small saucepan and set over medium heat. Warm until the butter has melted and the mixture is just starting to bubble. Remove from the heat and stir in the baking soda. Pour this mixture into the dry ingredients and stir quickly until just combined.

Put teaspoons of the mixture onto the prepared baking sheets, leaving some space in between them. (You may need to cook the dough in batches.) Bake in the preheated oven for about 10 minutes, until golden brown. Transfer to a wire rack to cool. Once cool, store in an airtight container and eat within 2–3 days.

wheat germ crisps with sesame seeds

These delicious crisp and buttery cookies have the added goodness of wheat germ, a tiny wheat seed that is extremely rich in proteins and vitamins. Wheat germ will only keep for a short period of time as its natural oil gradually becomes rancid stored at room temperature, so it should always be kept in the fridge in an airtight container and used before the best-before date.

1 stick plus 4 tablespoons unsalted butter, at room temperature
¾ cup plus 3 tablespoons natural cane sugar
1 egg, lightly beaten
3 tablespoons wheat germ
¼ cup sesame seeds
1 cup plus 2 tablespoons white whole-wheat flour
½ teaspoon baking powder

1–2 baking sheets lined with greaseproof paper

Makes about 36 cookies

Preheat the oven to 350°F.

Beat the butter and sugar until pale and creamy. Add the egg and beat for 1 minute more. Fold in the wheat germ, sesame seeds, flour, and baking powder until well combined.

Put teaspoons of the mixture onto the prepared baking sheets, leaving some space between them. (You may need to cook the mixture in several batches.)

Bake in the preheated oven for 12–15 minutes, until golden and crisp. Transfer to a wire rack to cool. Once cool, store in an airtight container and eat within 2 days.

oaty cookies

These simple cookies are not overly sweet and can be served as an accompaniment to a full-flavored cheese such as Parmesan, pecorino, or sharp cheddar. If you can buy Spanish quince paste (*membrillo*) or any other fruit preserve, try serving this alongside.

1¼ cups rolled oats
¼ cup packed light brown sugar
1½ cups whole-wheat flour
(white or regular)
1 teaspoon baking soda
½ teaspoon sea salt
1 stick unsalted butter, melted
¼ cup whole milk

1–2 baking sheets lined with baking parchment

a 2½ inch fluted cookie cutter

Makes about 36 cookies

Preheat the oven to 350°F.

Put the oats and sugar in a mixing bowl and sift in the flour, baking soda, and salt. Tip any husks from the strainer into the bowl.

Stir in the butter and milk to make a stiff dough. Briefly knead on a lightly floured work surface, then form into a ball and divide into two portions of equal size.

Roll each ball of dough out between two sheets of baking parchment until no thicker than ¼-inch. Use the cookie cutter to stamp out 18 cookies from each portion of dough.

Arrange the cookies on the prepared baking sheets and bake in the preheated oven for about 12 minutes, until pale golden. Transfer to a wire rack to cool. Once cool, store in an airtight container and eat within 2–3 days.

Variation: To make a spiced fruit cookie, add 2 oz. finely chopped dried apples or figs to the dry ingredients along with a pinch each of ground cinnamon and freshly grated nutmeg.

quinoa choc chip cookies

Although quinoa is most often used for stuffings, pilafs, and baked dishes, it is also sometimes used for breakfast cereals, so, just like oats it makes a great addition to these home-baked cookies. Use good dark chocolate chips full of antioxidants to turn these into a guilt-free treat, packed with nutritious ingredients, that is far superior to any cookie you can buy.

½ cup rolled oats
¾ cup quinoa
1 cup all-purpose flour
½ teaspoon baking powder
½ teaspoon baking soda
1 stick unsalted butter, at room temperature
½ cup demerara sugar
½ cup packed brown sugar
¾ cup premium semisweet or bittersweet chocolate chips

1–2 baking sheets lined with baking parchment

Makes about 24 cookies

Preheat the oven to 350°F.

Put the oats and quinoa in a food processor and process until finely chopped and the mixture resembles ground almonds. Transfer to a bowl and add the flour, baking powder, and baking soda. Mix to combine.

Put the butter and both sugars in a separate mixing bowl and beat for 4–5 minutes, until thick and pale. Stir in the dry ingredients to make a thick dough, then stir in the chocolate chips.

Put tablespoons of the dough onto the prepared baking sheets and bake in the preheated oven for 10 minutes, until golden. Transfer to a wire rack to cool. Once cool, store in an airtight container and eat within 2–3 days.

maple, coconut, and almond granola

This delicious granola can be enjoyed at breakfast time with fresh fruit and yogurt or as a nutritious snack. The cereal, nuts, and grains added are all simply thrown together and baked until golden. The inclusion of something sticky such as sugar, honey, or maple syrup as here, encourages the other ingredients to form themselves into irresistible chewy and crunchy clumps.

2½ cups organic whole oats

1 tablespoon almond oil

⅓ cup sesame seeds

¼ cup sunflower seeds

3 tablespoons wheat germ

⅓ cup unsweetened desiccated coconut

¼ cup flaked almonds

3 tablespoons pure maple syrup

3 tablespoons light brown sugar, sifted

Makes 4–6 servings

Preheat the oven to 350°F.

Put the oats and almond oil in a small roasting pan and cook in the preheated oven for 20 minutes, stirring every 5 minutes.

Remove from the oven and add the sesame seeds, sunflower seeds, and wheat germ. Return to the oven and cook for 10 minutes more, stirring after 5 minutes.

Remove from the oven and add the coconut and almonds. Return to the oven and cook for 8–10 minutes more, until the coconut is golden, stirring after 5 minutes.

Stir in the maple syrup until well combined, then sprinkle over the brown sugar. Return to the oven and cook for 5 minutes more, until the granola is toasted and an even golden color all over.

Let cool, then store in an airtight container for up to 5 days.

blueberry and apple muffins with bran

As I make muffins on a regular basis, I really appreciate a recipe that is simple and quick. The most important thing to remember when following any muffin recipe is not to overmix the dough. Use a large spoon to fold the ingredients together. You want it to look lumpy; if you end up with a smooth mixture it means your muffins will be tough.

1 cup buttermilk
¼ cup pure vegetable oil
3 cups all-purpose flour
⅓ cup unsweetened bran cereal (such as All-bran)
1 heaping tablespoon baking powder
1 small green eating apple, peeled, cored, and grated
1⅓ cups fresh or frozen blueberries
1 egg
⅔ cup natural cane sugar
butter or cream cheese, to serve

a 12-cup muffin pan, greased

Makes 12 muffins

Preheat the oven to 350°F.

Put the buttermilk in a pitcher. Add the oil and stir well to combine.

Put the flour, bran cereal, and baking powder in a mixing bowl and stir to combine. Add the grated apple and use your hands to combine the ingredients, separating the apple pieces and tossing to coat in the flour. Add the blueberries, and again use your hands to combine.

Put the egg and sugar in a separate bowl and whisk for 1 minute, until thick and pale. Add the buttermilk mixture and whisk to combine. Pour this into the dry ingredients and use a large metal spoon to gently fold together for a few seconds only, without overmixing.

Spoon the mixture into the prepared muffin pan, dividing evenly. Bake in the preheated oven for about 20 minutes, until risen and golden. Serve warm with butter or cream cheese. These are best eaten on the day they are baked.

easy banana bread

Think you can't bake? Well, you haven't tried this recipe. Make it on the morning you intend to eat it and fill the house with the seductive smell of cinnamon. Serve it warm spread with fresh ricotta and honey. Or make it a day or two in advance and lightly toast to serve.

¾ cup natural cane sugar
2 eggs
½ cup pure vegetable oil
2 bananas, peeled and mashed
2 cups white whole-wheat flour
1½ teaspoons baking powder
1 teaspoon ground cinnamon
fresh ricotta and honey, to serve (optional)

a 8 x 4 inch loaf pan, greased

Makes 1 medium loaf

Preheat the oven to 350°F.

Whisk the sugar and eggs together in a bowl. Stir in the oil and ¼ cup cold water until combined.

Stir in the mashed bananas, flour, baking powder, and cinnamon until just combined. Spoon into the prepared loaf pan and bake in the preheated oven for 50–55 minutes, until golden and firm on top. Let cool in the pan for 10 minutes before inverting onto a wire rack.

Serve warm on the day it is made or cooled and toasted, with ricotta and honey, if liked. The bread will keep for up to 2 days in an airtight container.

Variation: For a tasty banana and date bread, add 4 oz. chopped pitted dates to the dough. This dough also makes great muffins—just spoon the mixture into a greased 12-cup muffin pan and bake in a preheated oven at 350°F for 20–25 minutes, until risen and golden. Drizzle over a little honey while the muffins are still warm.

four-flour bread

This wholesome bread is very therapeutic to prepare—just give yourself some time to enjoy the process and not feel rushed. It's very rewarding to make on a weekend morning to enjoy for lunch with a comforting soup.

3½ cups whole-wheat flour (white or regular)
½ cup rye flour
½ cup spelt flour
½ cup soy flour
2 teaspoons sea salt
¼ cup organic whole oats
⅓ cup packed light brown sugar, plus 1 teaspoon
2 teaspoons dried yeast
⅓ cup rice bran oil

a 8 x 4 inch loaf pan, lightly greased

Makes 1 medium loaf

Sift all four of the flours and salt into a large mixing bowl. Stir in any husks from the strainer, the oats, and the ⅓ cup of sugar. Set aside.

Put the yeast and the 1 teaspoon of sugar in a small bowl and add ½ cup warm water. Cover and set aside in a warm place for about 10–15 minutes, until frothy and bubbling.

Add the yeast mixture, 1½ cups warm water and the oil to the flour mixture and stir well to combine. Cover and set aside in a warm place for about 30–45 minutes, until just risen slightly.

Preheat the oven to 425°F.

Knead the dough on a lightly floured surface for 8–10 minutes. Divide into two equal portions and form each into a ball. Sit each ball side by side in the prepared loaf pan. Cover and set aside in a warm place for 30 minutes. Lightly brush the top of the dough with water and bake in the preheated oven for 20 minutes. Reduce the oven temperature to 350°F and bake for 20–25 minutes more, until risen and golden and the loaf sounds hollow when tapped on the base. This bread is best eaten on the day it is made.

spicy cornbread

When corn is in season, cut the kernels from a fresh ear of corn and add to the batter after adding the eggs. I actually like to eat this for breakfast, toasted and served with scrambled eggs and salsa on the side, but it's a great side with a chili con carne. This freezes well, simply reheat in the oven before serving.

1¾ cups fine yellow cornmeal

½ cup all-purpose flour

1 teaspoon baking soda

2 teaspoons baking powder

1 teaspoon fine sea salt

1 teaspoon sugar

1 teaspoon dried hot pepper flakes

a handful of cilantro leaves, roughly chopped

1 cup buttermilk

½ cup light cream

6½ tablespoons unsalted butter

3 eggs, lightly beaten

a 8 x 12 inch baking pan, greased and lined with baking parchment

Makes about 16 pieces

Preheat the oven to 400°F.

Sift the cornmeal, flour, baking soda, baking powder, and salt into a large mixing bowl. Stir in the hot pepper flakes and cilantro and make a well in the center.

Put the buttermilk, cream, and butter into a small saucepan and set over low heat. Heat until the butter has just melted. Pour into the flour mixture along with the beaten eggs, stir quickly to combine, then pour into the prepared baking pan.

Bake in the preheated oven for 18–20 minutes, until golden. Let cool in the pan for 5 minutes, then lift out and cut into squares. Keep covered with a clean napkin and serve while still warm.

couscous and cashew nut soda bread

This was something of an experiment but thankfully one with delicious results! Don't worry if the mixture looks a bit wet—as it cooks the couscous expands to give you a nutty loaf that's light, fluffy, and easy to slice. Serve with dips, soups, or alongside any grazing platter.

2½ cups whole-wheat flour
(white or regular)
1 teaspoon baking soda
1 teaspoon baking powder
scant ½ cup couscous
⅔ cup salted cashew nuts,
roughly chopped
1 cup buttermilk

*a 8 x 4 inch loaf pan, lightly
greased with olive oil*

Makes about 16 pieces

Preheat the oven to 400°F.

Put the flour, baking soda, baking powder, couscous, and cashews in a large mixing bowl, making a well in the center.

Pour the buttermilk into the flour along with 1¾ cups warm water and stir quickly to combine.

Spoon the mixture into the prepared loaf pan and bake in the preheated oven for 45 minutes, until risen and golden on top.

Let cool in the pan for 10–15 minutes before removing. Slice and serve while still warm or serve cooled and toasted. The bread will keep for up to 2 days in an airtight container.

Lebanese rose and pistachio rice pudding

This delicious baked dessert makes use of floral and heady rosewater, a much-loved ingredient in Middle Eastern cooking—do go easy though, only a little is needed.

4 cups whole milk
1 cup short grain white rice
1 cup granulated sugar
1 egg yolk
2 tablespoons cornstarch
1–2 teaspoons rosewater, to taste
¼ cup whipping cream
½ teaspoon ground cinnamon
⅓ cup shelled unsalted pistachios, roughly chopped

Serves 4

Pour ¼ cup of the milk into a mixing bowl and set aside until needed.

Combine the remaining milk, rice, and sugar in a heavy-based saucepan and set over low/medium heat. Cook for about 45–50 minutes, stirring often, until the rice is just tender (ensuring that it does not catch on the bottom of the pan).

Add the egg yolk and cornstarch to the reserved milk and whisk until smooth. Slowly stir about ¼ cup of the hot rice mixture into the yolk mixture and then return this to the rice mixture. Stir well to combine, until the rice mixture has thickened. Remove from the heat and stir in the rosewater.

Set aside to cool. Meanwhile, whip the cream until softly peaking. Fold it into the cooled rice mixture and sprinkle with the cinnamon and pistachios. Serve at room temperature.

vanilla rice pudding

This is a traditional English rice pudding which is slow-cooked and develops a lovely golden skin on top. Feel free to add a handful of golden raisins and a little grated nutmeg for a simple variation.

1 vanilla bean
4 cups whole milk
½ cup light cream
½ stick unsalted butter
½ cup granulated sugar
½ cup short grain white rice

a medium flameproof baking dish

Serves 4

Preheat the oven to 300°F.

Roll the vanilla bean between the palms of your hand to soften. Split it lengthwise with a small sharp knife and use the tip of the knife to scrape the seeds directly into a bowl. Add the milk, cream, and sugar and whisk well to combine.

Put the butter in a medium, flameproof baking dish and set over high heat. When the butter is sizzling add the rice and stir for 1–2 minutes, until it is shiny and glossy. Carefully pour the milk mixture into the dish and use a large spoon to gently stir, breaking up any large lumps of rice and freeing any grains that are stuck to the bottom of the dish.

Transfer to the preheated oven and bake, uncovered, for 3 hours, until the top has a golden brown crust. Let cool slightly before serving.

chocolate and aduki bean paste phyllo fingers

Aduki beans are tiny, deep-red beans which have a sweet, nutty flavor and are more often used for sweet dishes than for savory ones. In Japan they are cooked, puréed, and mixed with sugar to make a paste which is used to fill cakes. It can be bought prepared but making it fresh is very easy and it tastes much better. It's not tooth-achingly sweet and is light on the palate after a meal, or simply enjoyed with a cup of green tea.

4 sheets phyllo dough

4 tablespoons unsalted butter, melted

½ quantity of homemade aduki bean paste (see recipe below) or a generous ½ cup prepared sweet aduki bean paste

4 oz. premium bittersweet chocolate, grated

2 tablespoons confectioners' sugar

aduki bean paste:

1 cup dried aduki beans

1 cup granulated sugar

a pinch of fine sea salt

a baking sheet lined with baking parchment

Makes about 8 fingers

To make the aduki bean paste, put the beans in a large, heavy-based saucepan and add enough cold water to cover them. Bring to a boil, then drain. Return the drained beans to the pan, add 3 cups cold water, and leave the beans to soak for 24 hours. (Discard any beans that remain floating.)

Bring the beans and soaking water to a boil, then reduce the heat and simmer for about 1 hour. Stir frequently with a wooden spoon until the beans are very soft and the water is almost absorbed. Add the sugar and stir. Add a pinch of salt, then transfer to a food processor and blend to a smooth paste.

Preheat the oven to 425°F.

Cut each sheet of phyllo dough in half lengthwise to give 8 pieces. Lay one of the pieces on a work surface and brush all over with the melted butter.

Put about 2 heaping teaspoons of the aduki bean paste in the center of the phyllo at the edge nearest you, making a mound about 2 inches long. Sprinkle over some of the chocolate. Roll the phyllo over to enclose the filling, fold in the sides, and continue rolling to form a log. Repeat to make 8 logs.

Arrange the phyllo fingers on the prepared baking sheet and bake in the preheated oven for 8–10 minutes, until golden and crisp. Dust lightly with confectioners' sugar and serve warm.

little almond, polenta, and lemon syrup cakes

Polenta is Italian cornmeal and it comes in various grades, ranging from coarse to fine—you want a very fine grade here (which you should be able to find at any Italian deli) for a good dense texture. It's best to eat these cakes on the day you make them, but that shouldn't be too difficult!

1 cup fine polenta

1 tablespoon baking powder

1¾ cups ground almonds

1 stick plus 6 tablespoons unsalted butter, at room temperature

1 cup natural cane sugar

1 tablespoon very finely grated lemon peel

4 eggs

lemon syrup:

½ cup granulated sugar

2 tablespoons freshly squeezed lemon juice

3 tablespoons flaked almonds, lightly toasted

confectioners' sugar, to serve

a 12-cup muffin pan, lightly greased

Makes 12 cakes

Preheat the oven to 350°F.

Sift the polenta, baking powder, and ground almonds into a large mixing bowl. Tip any pieces of husk into the bowl and make a well in the center.

In a separate bowl, beat the butter, sugar, and lemon peel together until pale and creamy. Add the eggs one at a time, beating well after each addition. Gradually fold in the polenta mixture until well combined.

Spoon the mixture into the prepared muffin pan, dividing evenly. Bake in the preheated oven for 25 minutes, until risen and golden. Remove from the oven and let cool in the pan for 10 minutes. Carefully transfer the cakes to a wire rack set over a baking sheet (to catch any drips of syrup.)

To make the syrup, put the sugar, lemon juice, and 2 tablespoons cold water in a small saucepan. Set over low heat and cook, stirring, until the sugar dissolves. Increase the heat to high and bring to a boil, then reduce the heat to a low simmer and cook for 2–3 minutes, until syrupy.

Pour the syrup over the warm cakes. Sprinkle the flaked almonds on top so they stick to the syrup. Let cool and dust with confectioners' sugar just before serving.

homemade semolina crumpets

The raising agent in crumpets is yeast and when the batter is exposed to the heat of the skillet, the air that is created by the yeast during its "proofing" expands and rises to the top of the crumpet, so they develop those distinctive little holes on top. These are densely textured crumpets and don't worry if the batter looks uncooked, as they are toasted before serving. Once upon a time you could buy specially-made crumpet rings but they are harder to find these days. Egg cooking rings do the job but must be very well greased before they are filled with batter.

1 cup bread flour
1 cup fine semolina
1 teaspoon granulated sugar
1 tablespoon dried yeast
about ½ stick unsalted butter, for frying

to serve:
fruit jam and whipped cream, or butter and honey

4 egg cooking rings, each about 3½–4 inches diameter, very well greased

Makes 8–10 crumpets

Put the flour, semolina, sugar, and yeast in the goblet of a blender. With the motor running, add 1⅓ cups warm water and continue to blend for 1 minute more. Scrape down the sides of the blender and blend for a further 30 seconds so the mixture is free of lumps. Pour into a large bowl, cover with plastic wrap and set aside in a warm place for 45–60 minutes, until the mixture is very frothy and bubbly.

Generously grease a heavy-based skillet (or cast iron griddle pan if you have one) with butter and set over high heat. Sit the prepared egg cooking rings in the pan and ladle about ½ cup of the crumpet mixture in each ring. Cook for 4–5 minutes, until bubbles form on the top and the sticky dough on the top has dried. Do not turn over. Transfer the cooked crumpets to a wire rack to cool and continue until all the batter has been used (regreasing the pan each time.)

Preheat the broiler to high. Lightly toast the tops of the crumpets, until golden. Serve hot with the fruit jam of your choice and whipped cream, or butter and honey, as preferred.

oaty apple and raisin crumble

A baked fruit crumble, served warm from the oven, has to be one of the most popular comfort foods. And the good news is that compared to most other desserts it is a healthy choice! I think that oats are a must in any crumble topping as they make for a deliciously crunchy texture.

2 tablespoons brandy
1 tablespoon honey
⅓ cup raisins (preferably flame)
5 Granny Smith apples, peeled cored and sliced
½ cup natural cane sugar
vanilla ice cream or chilled light cream, to serve

crumble topping:
⅔ cup regular whole-wheat flour
¼ cup rolled oats
½ teaspoon baking powder
½ teaspoon ground cinnamon
5 tablespoons unsalted butter, chilled and cut into pieces
5 tablespoons light brown or demerara sugar
vanilla ice cream or chilled light cream, to serve (optional)

a medium baking dish, buttered

Serves 4

Preheat the oven to 400°F.

Put the brandy, honey, and raisins in a small saucepan and set over medium heat. Cook for 5 minutes, stirring constantly, until almost all the liquid has evaporated. Set aside.

Put the apples, sugar, and 2 tablespoons cold water in a separate saucepan and set over medium heat. Cover and cook for about 10–15 minutes, stirring often, until the apples have softened. Stir in the raisin mixture and let cool. Transfer to the prepared baking dish.

To make the crumble topping, put the flour, oats, baking powder, cinnamon, and butter in a bowl. Use your hands to combine all of the ingredients, rubbing the butter between your fingertips, until the mixture resembles coarse sand. Stir in the brown sugar and sprinkle the mixture evenly over the apple mixture in the baking dish.

Bake in the preheated oven for 25–30 minutes, until the topping is crisp and golden. Serve warm with vanilla ice cream or cold cream, as preferred.

honeyed couscous with fresh figs and rosewater cream

In Morocco, sweet couscous is one of the most popular snacks and is also enjoyed as a nourishing breakfast, served with a variety of dried fruits and nuts and plenty of honey and cream for pouring. This is my take on the traditional recipe and makes a deliciously different and indulgent dessert.

1 cup couscous
1 tablespoon unsalted butter
2 tablespoons honey
½ teaspoon ground cinnamon
4–6 fresh figs, halved
1 teaspoon natural cane sugar
½ cup heavy cream
2 tablespoons light brown sugar
½ teaspoon rosewater

Serves 4

Put the couscous in a heatproof bowl and set aside.

Put the butter, honey, cinnamon, and ½ cup cold water in a small saucepan and set over high heat. As soon as the mixture boils pour it over the couscous, quickly stir just to combine, and cover tightly with plastic wrap. Let sit for 10 minutes, then fluff up with a fork, making certain to pick up the grains at the bottom of the bowl. Re-cover and let sit for 5–10 minutes more. When cool enough to handle, use your fingertips to fluff and separate the grains for a light-as-air texture.

Preheat the broiler to high. Sprinkle the cane sugar over the cut sides of the figs and cook under the broiler, until the sugar is golden and the figs have softened just slightly.

Put the cream, brown sugar, and rosewater in a small bowl and stir to combine.

To serve, spoon the couscous into serving bowls, arrange a few fig halves on top, and add a spoonful of the rosewater cream. Serve immediately.

spiced oatmeal cake with chocolate and cinnamon frosting

This is a dense and richly spiced cake and not one for the fainthearted. It is smothered with a finger-licking ganache of chocolate and cream which is good enough to eat on its own but do try and save some for the cake!

⅔ cup rolled oats

1 stick unsalted butter, at room temperature

2¼ cups packed light brown sugar

1 cup granulated sugar

2 eggs

1⅓ cups all-purpose flour

1 teaspoon baking powder

1 teaspoon ground cinnamon

¼ teaspoon freshly grated nutmeg

cinnamon chocolate frosting:

¾ cup light cream

6 oz. premium bittersweet chocolate, broken into pieces

½ teaspoon ground cinnamon

a springform cake pan, 8 inches diameter, lightly greased and lined with parchment paper

Serves 10–12

Preheat the oven to 350°F.

Put the oats in a heatproof bowl. Add 1¼ cups boiling water and stir. Cover with plastic wrap and let sit for 20 minutes.

Put the butter and both sugars in a mixing bowl and beat together until pale, thick, and creamy.

Add one of the eggs and beat until well combined. Add the remaining egg and beat again. Stir in the flour, baking powder, cinnamon, and nutmeg, then fold in the softened oats. Spoon the mixture into the prepared cake pan and level the surface.

Bake in the preheated oven for 35–40 minutes, until golden. Let cool in the pan for 10 minutes, then transfer to a wire rack to cool completely.

To make the frosting, set a heatproof bowl over a saucepan of barely simmering water, making certain the boiling water does not come into contact with the bottom of the bowl. Pour the cream into the bowl and let it warm slightly. Add the chocolate and cinnamon and stir constantly until the chocolate has melted and the mixture is dark and smooth.

Remove from the heat and let cool for about 30 minutes, until the frosting is a thick, spreading consistency. Use a palette knife or spatula to spread the frosting evenly over the sides and top of the cake. Cut into slices to serve. The cake will keep in an airtight container for 2–3 days.

index

conversion chart

Weights and measures have been rounded up
or down slightly to make measuring easier.

Volume equivalents:

American	Metric	Imperial
6 tbsp butter	85 g	3 oz.
7 tbsp butter	100 g	3½ oz.
1 stick butter	115 g	4 oz.
1 teaspoon	5 ml	
1 tablespoon	15 ml	
¼ cup	60 ml	2 fl.oz.
⅓ cup	75 ml	2½ fl.oz.
½ cup	125 ml	4 fl.oz.
⅔ cup	150 ml	5 fl.oz. (¼ pint)
¾ cup	175 ml	6 fl.oz.
1 cup	250 ml	8 fl.oz.

Oven temperatures:

120°C/130°C	(250°F)	Gas ½
140°C	(275°F)	Gas 1
150°C	(300°F)	Gas 2
160°C/170°C	(325°F)	Gas 3
180°C	(350°F)	Gas 4
190°C	(375°F)	Gas 5
200°C	(400°F)	Gas 6
220°C	(425°F)	Gas 7

Weight equivalents:		**Measurements:**	
Imperial	Metric	Inches	Cm
1 oz.	30 g	¼ inch	0.5 cm
2 oz.	55 g	½ inch	1 cm
3 oz.	85 g	¾ inch	1.5 cm
3½ oz.	100 g	1 inch	2.5 cm
4 oz.	115 g	2 inches	5 cm
5 oz.	140 g	3 inches	7 cm
6 oz.	175 g	4 inches	10 cm
8 oz. (½ lb.)	225 g	5 inches	12 cm
9 oz.	250 g	6 inches	15 cm
10 oz.	280 g	7 inches	18 cm
11½ oz.	325 g	8 inches	20 cm
12 oz.	350 g	9 inches	23 cm
13 oz.	375 g	10 inches	25 cm
14 oz.	400 g	11 inches	28 cm
15 oz.	425 g	12 inches	30 cm
16 oz. (1 lb.)	450 g		

WITHDRAWN